Carrott the Handyman
'I once put up wallpaper with Polyfilla. It vaguely occurred to me how expensive it was putting up a couple of rolls: about £100 . . .'

Carrott the Man of the World
'I'd always thought sado-masochism was a disease you suffered in old age!'

Carrott and The Orgy
'All the guys are in an alcoholic daze . . . all standing with drinks in their hands and trousers around their ankles'

Carrott and Photographers
'Every photographer always starts by getting out a carrot with his camera. I've had carrots up my nose, in my ears, I've had them chewed, grated, cubed, mashed . . .'

The Zit-Kid
'What are you doing in the bathroom, Jasper?'

Also in Arrow by Jasper Carrott
Sweet and Sour Labrador

A Little Bit on the Side

Jasper Carrott

Text illustrations by David English

ARROW BOOKS

Arrow Books Limited
62-65 Chandos Place, London WC2N 4NW

An imprint of Century Hutchinson Ltd

London Melbourne Sydney Auckland
Johannesburg and agencies throughout
the world

First published 1979
Reprinted 1979 (three times), 1980 (seven times),
1981 (four times), 1983 (three times), 1984 (twice),
1985 (twice) and 1986

© Jasper Carrott 1979
Text illustrations © Arrow Books Ltd 1979

This book is sold subject to the condition that it shall not, by
way of trade or otherwise, be lent, resold, hired out, or
otherwise circulated without the publisher's prior consent in
any form of binding or cover other than that in which it is
published and without a similar condition including this
condition being imposed on the subsequent purchaser

Set in VIP Baskerville

Printed and bound in Great Britain by
Anchor Brendon Limited, Tiptree, Essex

ISBN 0 09 921700 7

Contents

Introduction	9
1 THE MISFIT	11
Schooldays	12
The Beehive	15
Summer holiday	19
Tweedle-Dum and Tweedle-Dee	22
2 MAKING IT (OR TRYING TO)	25
Bottled up	26
Television repairman	28
Bev Bevan, handyman	31
3 DEATH OF A SALESMAN	35
Task Force Carrott	36
Roy Wood, salesmen's dream	41
Biffer the dog	43
Arthur the hamster	46
4 THE ROAD TO REDDITCH	49
Caught-ing	50
Bognor to The Boggery	52
Scunthorpe Baths	55
John Starkey, the collector	58
VAT-man	60
5 SOCCER GROUPIE	63
Sunday football	64
"ello Tone, 'arry 'ere'	68
Villa Parkers	71
Motor spares man	73

6	THE WEDDING	77
7	FOREIGNERS AND OTHER PROBLEMS	83
	The Italian job	84
	The Cyprus connection	88
	RAF bases	90
	Sudden death in the greyhound stadium	91
8	PERSONAL APPEARANCES AND MORE DISASTERS	95
	This ain't Shakespeare	96
	W(V)arrington	100
	Coronation Street meets Crossroads	102
9	WE LIKE IT – BUT IT WILL NEVER SELL	105
	'Magic Roundabout'	106
	'Top of the Pops'	110
	Colin Slade, walking dynamo	114
	Jester Carrott	116
10	THE OTHER SIDE OF THE CAMERA	119
	Smile, please!	120
	Scarface	122
11	FROM MOTORWAYS TO MOLES	125
	Motorway chefs	126
	The wine expert	128
	The Girt Clog Climbing Club	129
	Sex supermarket	131
	Mole-in-the-hole	132
12	ON THE BUSES	137
	Dial-a-Bus	138
	Insurance forms	139
	Whisky bottle	141
	The Nutter	143

13 DRIVEN TO DISTRACTION	**147**
Driver-in-law	148
Parking ticket	150
Jersey	152
The boys in blue	154
14 AMERICAN DREAM	**157**
Rent-a-wreck	158
B-o-l-l-o-c-k-s	160

Introduction

All the characters in this book are entirely non-fictitious and any reference to people, dead or alive, is purely intentional.

It's all my own work apart from pages 1 to 160 where I was aided and abetted by Garth Pearce, novelist and *Daily Express* showbusiness writer. If anyone is offended by the nature of the book, just think how I feel!

Jasper Carrott

1 The Misfit

Schooldays

I went through my entire schooldays totally undiscovered. An absolute nonentity. I only had my name in the school magazine once and that was when they printed all the first-formers.

When you were in the first form did you used to have fagging? Everyone would pick on you. We had this thing at our school called 'the blue goldfish'.

'Have you seen the blue goldfish?'

The first-formers would shake their heads dumbly: 'Nooo. . . .'

'Would you like to see it?'

'Yees. . . .'

They would then take you to the lavatory, point down and say: 'There it is.'

The unsuspecting first-former, in his new uniform, cap and tie, would then bend down to look and 'wooosh' – the chain was pulled and he would be doused with several gallons of Armitage's best from the toilet basin.

I never twigged what it was about and up until the fifth form I was still looking for the blue goldfish. My mother always thought it rained a lot at our school.

I have always had this total trust in other people.

The first time I played rugby was at Moseley Grammar School in the first form. It was also the first time we'd had to get changed in front of everybody. In the junior school you kept your trousers on. But here . . . you were at the senior school and a big lad.

These couple of prefects came in to the changing

room, started wandering round and came up to me: 'Played rugby before, mate?'

'Er, no.'

'It ain't half a rough sport, you know. Blood, guts, gore. . . .'

'Gulp!'

'You need plenty of protection. You got any protection?'

'Er. . . .'

'Well you ought to be wearing a box, you know. You got a box?'

'No.'

They happened to have one with them, didn't they? I was told all about it and then was last on to the pitch. The first time I ever played rugby in my life, in front of all the first form, the masters and the prefects. I'd got this cricket box on my nose. . . .

I must admit, it did smell odd. I thought: 'I wonder where this bloke's had his nose.'

I suppose my only real contribution to school life was the insect race during what was called Activity Week.

I suggested the race, and it was quickly agreed because everyone else thought that as it was my idea they could leave me to supply the insects.

The race was due on a Thursday, and on the Wednesday night I had to go round the garden frantically trying to find insects. I got a fantastic beetle which used to whizz along. It was so fast I had to crush one of its legs to try and slow it down. I also found a spider and a dozen wood lice.

Our form master was a guy called Fletcher who was also the school's carpentry teacher. He said that we could have the carpentry room to organize the insect race. He'd got his blackboard, put rings on it in chalk and had placed it flat on the ground. The first insect to make the outer chalk mark was the winner.

A large crowd had gathered with expectant apathy.

As soon as I turned over the pot of insects the beetle made straight for the edge, while the wood lice pottered around in the middle. The spider didn't move at all, due to a large chunk of its abdomen being eaten by the beetle.

It took about 3/10 of a second for everyone to realize that this was *extremely* uninteresting. In fact, in the entire school it was probably the most boring event of the Activity Week.

The wood lice just went round and round in the centre of the blackboard and everyone vaguely wandered off, including me. The beetle took off altogether and the spider appeared to be dead.

Yet when I returned to collect the wood lice I only found two. I think to this day Moseley Grammar School must wonder how they have managed to rear an army of the fattest wood lice in history in their carpentry room. . . .

I estimate the entire building has about another five years left.

The Beehive

I managed to get two GCE 'O' levels in maths and art. There's not a lot you can do in life with those, apart from paint computers.

Now there was a department store in Birmingham called The Beehive which had been in existence since about 1875. The people who worked there had either been there since its opening or were misfits. For some reason it used to attract every misfit salesperson in the city.

When I was still at school having interviews with the career officer I didn't have much idea of what to do. The career officer had even less idea than I did. His main objective was to get rid of me as fast as possible so he could get stuck into some real swats – those with four 'O' levels. I'd put down 'electrical engineer' because my uncle said I looked like one – but I hadn't got any 'O' levels in science. Under pressure, I vaguely told him that I might like to be a salesman and his eyes lit up. I could see him thinking: 'Misfit-Beehive!'

Exactly the same thing happened to Bev Bevan, now the drummer for Electric Light Orchestra. We used to sit next to each other in class and had managed to muster four 'O' levels between us.

So Bev, me and another kid called 'Wongy' Wheelan were selected as the only victims from our school for The Beehive. Wongy looked like a Chinaman and had a sister who looked identical. The only difference between them was the length of their hair. The strange thing about Wongy was that he married a girl who looked more like him than his sister did! An ace misfit if ever I saw one. He had loads of time off school and was always bringing false letters from his mum which he had written himself. Then one day he brought in a genuine letter because he really had been ill. They accused him of writing it himself. When they actually found out that his mother *had* written it and he'd written the rest from the previous three years they expelled him. Wongy had managed to get one 'O' level in religious knowledge....

It was a store packed with losers.

There was an ex-army captain as salesman in the kitchen furniture department whose attitude to life was that the younger generation had gone to pot. Looking back in retrospect I reckon there were a few ageing homosexuals around, too, because I was always having my bum pinched. And the women! Bumps on their shoulders and varicose veins.

The lift attendant, Tony, was a paraplegic. He was in an Express lift – one of those like a cage which was hand-operated. We instantly called it the Tony Express. Now Tony had a lovely sense of humour, but as a lift attendant he had his limitations. He had no co-ordination at all. When the lift was going up and down between the floors he had to try and stop it manually. The tension in the springs had gone years ago and having stopped the lift it would be a full minute before it finished wobbling up and down like a yo-yo. But it would take five attempts before he could get the lift level. So a journey from the haberdashery to the stationery departments would take a full half-hour. You could hear the cries of these old biddies echoing around the store: 'Help. Let me out. Let me out.' He would then open the gates and they would be about two feet off the ground, which is the nearest he came to being level. Shop assistants were forever rushing forward to help these old biddies, who would be clutching the bars of the lift and staring wild-eyed like inmates of a death cell. If Tony was having a bad day, step-ladders would have to be called for.

The planner from the kitchen department was like Mister Magoo. He couldn't see a thing. He would take his glasses off to look at plans and stick them right up to his nose. The thing about his fitted kitchens was that nothing *ever* fitted.

Then there was the toy department and a children's grotto in the basement, which was windowless. It was frightening and pokey and a big boiler was going zung ... zung ... zung ... all day long. The grotto was called 'Hansel and Gretel' and was really scarey. Even the staff didn't like going near it. The kids would come out screaming. Worse than any ghost train at a fair.

At the end of the grotto was a senile Father Christmas who was in residence from about the end of October up until Christmas Eve. He was always fine in the morning, but he'd come back after lunch as pissed as a fart. He would spend hours talking to these kids: what did they want; where had they been for their summer holidays; what was their favourite colour? Queues used to form round the block. We used to say, 'Come on, hurry up Father Christmas, there's thousands waiting to get in here.' The trouble was after ten minutes of breathing in his alcoholic fumes the kids would be as pissed as he was.

If that wasn't enough, there was a lucky dip for half a crown, which consisted of a really awful pen and pencil set. Parents used to bring them back within the week because they either wouldn't work or had snapped altogether. So on Saturday there would be a pissed Father Christmas, a queue forming up the stairs as he tried to get a life story out of every child who sat on his knee, kids screaming because they were petrified of the fairy grotto, eight year-olds staggering around demanding more alcohol, and dads creating because they'd been ripped off with this lousy pen and pencil set in a plastic holder, which was supposed to be a train or a pillar-box (no one was too sure).

The store would employ salesmen who had physical disabilities and always put them to work in the china department. One guy whose hands wouldn't work properly was given the job of wrapping the purchases. You could hear yells and crashes on the floor all day.

The only place that did really well was the bedding department.

The bedding department overlooked this stationery room on the other side of the street. You would often see a couple having it off over there at obscure times . . . half a bum going up and down because of a curtain pulled across the window which wouldn't quite reach. Crowds would form! And while they were viewing this bum it would give us a chance to sell them a bed.

The store's sign-writer was French. He'd be sitting reading for most of the day in his office. But as the books were in French no one could understand them. It was only when we took on somebody who could actually read French – a miracle in itself – did we discover they were pornographic. We should have realized because he used to wear ties with nudes on. And every time a salesgirl went in with a new price sign she wanted writing you would hear a strangled scream: 'Oooh, no . . . stop it!' They would come out dishevelled but with a slight grin on their face. It was only an ageing French pervert who would ever consider molesting any girl from the Beehive.

Summer holiday

By the time I was seventeen I'd have done anything to escape The Beehive.

I think that's why I decided to take a holiday abroad. Now the only holidays I had been on up to this point were two visits to the YMCA on Barry Island. But this time I'd got a scooter Lambretta 150cc (wow!) and my intention was to get a ferry from Dover, go to Ostend and travel to Sweden – all in two weeks. The furthest I'd been on the Lambretta was Stratford-upon-Avon and the top speed was forty-seven miles an hour.

I eventually found this mate mad enough to go with me. He was six foot four inches tall and as thin as a beanstalk. I was five feet eleven inches and also very thin at the time. And we had luggage piled about five feet high on the back of the scooter.

My parents looked sick with worry as we waved them good-bye. I always remember them looking at us as we set off – almost as if they would never see me again.

We travelled for three solid hours in pouring rain and got as far as Northampton. By then I was heartily sick of the whole idea of a Continental trip. When we hit London it took us *hours* to find a way out of it again. At 2 a.m. we were still lost in Soho. Twenty miles the other side we broke down at exactly five o'clock in the morning.

As I'd had some foresight to join the AA we got one of their men to come out: 'You've got as much chance of reaching Sweden as I have of going to Moscow,' he said. But he managed to get the thing going again and we just about reached Ostend.

One of the girls who worked at The Beehive had insisted that we stay the night with her parents who lived in Ostend. She had written to them and had given us their address.

When we turned up her parents took one look at us – two beanstalk ginks standing in front of a steaming Lambretta, perilously piled high with enough luggage for an attempt at Everest. (I'm sure at one stage they were looking for the sherpas.) They immediately and most strenuously denied all knowledge of us, the letter, their daughter, The Beehive and even their own language.

We finally found a room for the night in a knackered place run by a seemingly innocent old woman. She conned us in to sharing a bed and then charged us seven quid for one night. We'd only brought fifteen pounds with us for the whole two weeks.

After that, it went from bad to worse.

It was youth hostels all along the line. At one place in Germany two English girls arrived and I heard one of them say, 'Oh, there's two English boys here. It would be nice if we could meet up with them.' One was quite good-looking, but the other wasn't much. There's always a Tom and Jerry, isn't there?

I always used to get the 'mouse' on every dance floor. Remember the 'don't like yours' bit? Well, that was me. A lot of people used to be very insistent that I went to discos with them, and it took me a long time to realize that I *always* ended up with the ugly one.

But I reckoned I stood a great chance here because I was with a mate who looked more gormless than me. It took me the rest of the holiday to get over the fact that *he* ended up with the good-looker.

He really thought he was John Surtees on this Lambretta after that.

But within twenty-four hours he took a bend so fast

we ran out of road. All the one side of my leg was like a butcher's shop, and we were really shaken up. I got on to the scooter to drive and the handlebars were about thirty degrees to the left. So there were the two of us, a six foot four white-faced jelly hanging grimly on to the back of a dance-floor reject, with blood oozing out of his jeans, driving along with handlebars pointing towards the kerb with about three ton of luggage on the back.

When we limped up to the next youth hostel the warden greeted me with a pack of thirteen and fourteen year-olds at his heels who seemed to take delight at our pain. The warden grinned as he got out the iodine to slap on my leg. He stared me straight in the eye as he did so and his young cronies were straining to get a look. I was determined not to flinch. I had before me an ageing Hitler Youth, determined to inflict revenge for his country's defeat. It was a battle of sheer courage. This was El Alamein all over again.

England lost.

Tweedle-Dum and Tweedle-Dee

I think it was that experience which today makes me so sympathetic to losers on holiday. I'll talk to *anybody*. If I'm in a hotel in Spain and see a couple huddled in a corner being ignored I *have* to go and talk to them.

Now Bev Bevan – we're still big mates and he and his wife often come away with us – is totally the opposite. He treats them as if they have the plague. I always look at them and think: Well, they can't be that bad. But they always are. They are usually incredibly boring and once I've made contact they're round my neck for the fortnight.

On this one holiday there was this couple of blokes in the hotel whom we'd christened Tweedle-Dum and Tweedle-Dee. One had buck teeth, pebble glasses and wore tweed jackets; the other was in bright coloured T-shirts but was extremely fat. After two weeks they were whiter than when they arrived.

Bevan gave them a glance and instantly knew: A Plague Job.

Me? I felt sorry for them, probably because I once was a Tweedle-Dum. But for Bevan's sake, I decided to keep clear.

They kept on saying 'hello' to me and after a couple of days I just had to say 'hello' back. That's all ... 'hello'.

'Hello,' they said. 'Where have you been today?'

You can't ignore that, so I said: 'We've just been round the cove.'

After that there was no getting away. Forty-five minutes standing on one foot and another trying to end the conversation, with Bevan looking down from the balcony holding his head in his hands.

We had to spend the rest of the holiday laying brilliantly prepared plots to try and avoid them. It was more strain than work.

We just about managed it. Then the next year we were waiting at Elmdon Airport to go to Ibiza and we heard a 'Hello'. There they were again – waiting to go out on the same plane!

2 Making It (or Trying To)

Bottled up

I was always looking for ways of making money to escape The Beehive.

One night I met this mate in a pub and he'd got a table lamp with him which he'd made from a VAT 69 whisky bottle. He had coated it with a solution and covered it in different coloured bits of gravel. He'd then sprayed it, put a hole in the bottom, threaded a wire through and put a shade on top. Looked very impressive. He had also done the same thing with a Courvoisier and Mateus Rosé bottle.

He asked me, because I was a salesman, how much they'd be worth.

So I took them round a few wholesalers and they estimated thirty bob each. I could hear the chinking of cash. I went back to my mate: 'You going to make more of these?'

'No.'

'How much stuff have you got left to spray the bottles?'

'Loads.'

The first thing I had to do was get some bottles.

I knew a guy in Smethwick who collected empties from pubs, and I went and ordered 500 VAT 69, Courvoisier and Mateus Rosé bottles from him at threepence each. I loaded up a car with these bottles and took them home to stack by the garage.

Within a day the dustmen had taken the lot!

I was on the phone to the council all afternoon trying to trace them while everyone at the other end denied all knowledge. Finally they had to admit:

'Okay, we took them. But they *were* near the dustbins.'

I had to wait ages for another load of bottles, but I'd got three women lined up to do the work for me. They had the bottles, loads of grit, cement and solution and set it all up in this mate's lounge. They had to slap the solution on the bottles, throw gravel at them and paint them like the beautiful originals.

I went back the next day and these things were God-awful. Great big gobs of cement hanging off and a multiple of shapes and colours. I salvaged about a hundred from their efforts and tried to sell them.

Then the complaints started to come in. . . . The bottles had gouged out people's sideboards, wouldn't stand up straight, bits started to come off them and they'd become top-heavy.

In the end I took the perfect bottle this bloke had originally made to a wholesaler and told him they were all the same. I left him four crateloads, took the money and scooted out. The last thing I saw was him crouched over one of these crates trying to figure out what possible connection there was between the contents and the original lamp I had taken in.

Television repairman

Little wonder, really, that I got involved with a con-man.

He would never talk in less than millions of pounds. Didn't know – or want to know – £25 or £30 profit. Would I be interested in a job? He had this 'fantastic' scheme . . . television repairs.

'But I don't know a thing about televisions,' I said.

'Oh, you don't have to know anything about *televisions*,' he said.

He was in an office next to a genuine television repair man. The con-man advertised in the local evening paper and when anyone called to say they'd got a faulty TV he would go out in a plain van, wearing a white coat, to the house. I went with him, also in a white coat.

The owner would tell him what was going wrong with their TV: fuzzy picture, no sound, that sort of thing. Now, remember, this guy knew *nothing* about televisions. He could put the plug in the socket, but that's about all.

Whatever was wrong with the TV he would get out a very impressive array of tools, take off the back and put a screwdriver in just the right place to produce a spark. Then he'd shake his head, whistle and say: 'We'll have to take this in. The output tranny transformer has got a vertical pole!'

The point being he *had* to get that television out of the house. The whole idea was to get it back to the genuine repair man, charge about three times the going rate to cover the costs of transport and his own profit, and then return the set.

Because we were in white coats and had screwdrivers in our hands no one would turn a hair or question our authority as we carted out their £300 colour telly into an unmarked van.

The next day he would telephone them with an inflated price and the *real* reason for its breakdown.

'What if you come across someone who knows what he's doing?' I asked.

'You won't,' he says. 'They wouldn't call *me* if they knew what they were doing.'

He would also sell them insurance to cover all TV repairs for £11 a year.

There would be the obvious calls: 'You know that eleven-pound insurance you sold us? Well, our tube's gone and needs replacing.'

'Of course, sir. It is completely guaranteed, and we shall replace it. No problem. Will you be in during the next hour?'

'Yes, I'll stay in.'

'Right, sir. I'll send one of my men round.'

Then he'd put the phone down and do absolutely nothing about it.

If the phone rang again he would hold his nose and say: 'Sketchley Dry Cleaners here. Sorry, wrong number!'

Four hours with him was enough for me.

I left him taking another call: 'I know we said we'd be round . . . we're short staffed . . . yes, the man's had pleurisy . . . look, don't call me that . . . you just come round . . . yes, you just do that . . . try it on . . . what do you want for bloody eleven pounds?'

I'm hopeless with televisions.

I rented a set once which after five days lost the colour picture.

I called the firm and a man was sent around the same morning. All he did was turn the tuning button and I had perfect colour.

'Oh, I am sorry,' said I, feeling embarrassed.

But about a week later the colour went again.

The same man arrives: 'You've tried the tuning button?'

'Yes,' I said, 'and there's still no picture.'

'Right.'

He touches the tuning button and within seconds there's a colour picture. It was weird. I'd been trying all morning to do it.

He spent ten minutes checking over the set and couldn't find anything wrong at all: 'It's a perfect set, sir.'

'I *am* sorry about this.'

'It's all right, sir. It's all right. Now you are *sure* you know how to operate this tuning button?'

'Definitely.'

Three days later and the set goes wrong again. This time there's no sign of a picture and only a loud crackling sound. I can't go wrong *this* time.

The same man arrives and there was no trace of a smile on his face this time. He was speaking through gritted teeth. I was hoping that there was something really major gone wrong, just so he'd go away happy.

'What's wrong *this* time, sir?'

I breathed a sigh of relief as the picture remained dormant and he got out his set of tools and opened the back. Then he suddenly seizes on a wire and I hear him catch his breath before speaking very slowly: 'Do you know what this is, sir?'

It was the aerial – it had simply fallen out from the back of the television.

I could have kicked the set in. Anything, in fact, to make it go genuinely wrong.

'I bet you think I'm a right dick, don't you?'

'No, sir,' he says. 'Not at all, sir.'

Bev Bevan, handyman

But although I'm a hopeless handyman I think Bev Bevan is even worse.

His wife lives in terror most of the time. She even calls in the television people to change channels.

He always holds his drumsticks as if they are sledgehammers and pounds those skins as if they're about to leap up and attack him. That's what he's like all the time. He never uses a nail unless it's less than six inches long and never uses anything but a hammer on *any* repair job. That guy would even change a plug with a hammer. It's a wonder he's got a stick of furniture left in his house.

I have this running battle with him over who is the worst.

I once put up wallpaper with Polyfilla. It vaguely occurred to me how expensive it was putting up a couple of rolls: about £100!

On our first house we had some carpets laid and the guy said: 'Do you want your doors cut?' I said: 'Is that in the price?'

'No. It's fifteen shillings a door.'

'Forget it. I'll do it myself.'

I took off the toilet door and then the bathroom door and, using a six-inch ruler, I estimated how much I needed to cut off.

I did the bathroom door first, but didn't cut enough off. It ended up dragging along the carpet so much you couldn't open it more than a few inches to squeeze through.

Disillusioned by this, I decided not to put the toilet door back on. I used it instead for pasting wallpaper in the lounge. Not that the wallpapering was very good: it was at an angle of 45 degrees to the skirting board. People thought they were leaning sideways when they were in our lounge.

For years we had no door on the toilet which was right at the top of the stairs. If we had visitors and they wanted to use it, no one could go out into the hall in case they were embarrassed. We had to put a 'vacant–engaged' sign on the inside of the lounge door.

When we came to sell the house I thought I'd better put the toilet door back on again. But by this time, being the awful handyman I was, I had lost the six-inch ruler. So I used knicker elastic to measure how much would have to come off.

I sawed so much off that when I put it back on it was like a Western saloon door. You would look up from the hall and see trousers around ankles when anyone was using the loo.

And when prospective buyers came to the house I used chewing gum to make sure the toilet door was open all the time, so they didn't have a chance to see it. But that escapade had its uses. Now my wife won't let me touch anything around the house, which is fine by me.

3 Death of a Salesman

Task Force Carrot

I finally fled The Beehive to become a Task Force Salesman. Or, at least, that's what the firm called me. There were four of us, plus a team leader, and we would drive all over the country trying to sell new products in small shops.

We would drive around in convoy: really flash, doing three-two formations on the M6. A bit like the Red Arrows of the sales force. We used to have contests to see who could get from Birmingham to Norwich the fastest; you would really lose face if you didn't go across traffic lights when they were on amber.

In fourteen months we had a total of twenty-seven accidents between the five of us (true). I think at one point they actually ran out of claim forms at head office. We were in convoy in Liverpool on a really icy day when the Task Force leader's car was trying to squeeze ahead of a lorry, decided he couldn't make it and pulled up sharply. THUMP - THUMP - THUMP - THUMP. In one day we'd got five claim forms to fill in! The three in the middle had got front *and* rear damage. We were witnesses to each other's accident, which was blamed upon a cyclist with a flat tyre.

Head office immediately dispatched someone to see what was going on, and he made us line up these cars. They looked like something out of World War Two. He went absolutely spare. Our jobs were on the line and he wanted to see us at five o'clock sharp! We went through our schedules and sales in double-quick time that day, filling out all the right forms and turning up dead on time.

But he was forty minutes late – he'd run into the back of a bread van.

We were given twenty-five shillings a night allowance while we were on the road, but always sought somewhere for less than a pound.

In Nottingham we found this guest house run by an old music hall lady. Obviously she'd been a singer but was getting on a bit now. Fat and brassy and blonde. And she checked us in wearing a negligee.

There was this very unsavoury-looking character who lived there, and when we got back one tea-time we could hear this awful row.

The landlady emerged from a room in tears saying: 'That awful man – he's awful.'

'But who is he?' we ask.

'He's a friend who just stays here.'

Then she starts: 'He's after my cigarettes. I bought him some this morning, he's smoked them and he's not having any more.'

We're getting on with our order books and not taking much notice, but suddenly he bursts into the room and bawls: 'Where's my cigarettes?'

'They're not your cigarettes,' she says. 'I bought yours this morning – these are mine.'

He shouts: 'I want those cigarettes! Are you gonna give me those cigarettes?'

She's cowering and not replying. He looks long and hard at us and storms out of the room.

'Awful man,' she says. 'He also drinks. It's terrible. He drinks more than he smokes.'

A couple of minutes later he barges in again: 'I want those cigarettes!'

'They're mine.'

He looks at us: 'I've asked her for those cigarettes, haven't I?' We nod. 'And she won't give them to me, will she?' We shake our heads. 'I've given her one last chance and she still won't give them to me.' He then crashes out of the room again.

Now this landlady has a dog called Huckleberry and at this point he pads in. She picks up the dog and hugs him hysterically: 'He drinks worse than he smokes, you know. Awful man! Awful.'

Seconds later he's at the door: 'She wouldn't give me those cigarettes, would she?'

We were saying in unison: 'No.'

'I've given her the last chance?'

'Yes.'

'Right!' Then he throws a whip into the room.

It was a leopard skin whip with about eight thongs on it. It landed in the middle of the carpet and there was silence. This landlady went absolutely crimson. So crimson I thought she was going to burst.

He finally growls: 'I warned her . . .' then marches off into the night.

Now I'm twenty years old and as green as a berry and I go and pick up the whip. The landlady is squeezing Huckleberry so tightly his eyes are almost shooting out of his head. And she looks as if she's turning a purple colour.

I ask innocently: 'He never hits you with this, does he?'

She snatches it off me and hides it under a cushion: 'No,' she says. 'He beats Huckleberry with it.'

Only later, at the pub, did the others tell me what it was all about. I'd always thought sado-masochism was some disease you suffered in old age!

We get back much later to see the guy arriving totally drunk and as gentle as a lamb. She grabs him, beats him very hard around the head with the whip and shoves him upstairs.

Some of those places we stayed. . . . In Bristol this

one joint served us a meal – it was usually used by out-of-work actors – and there was a fly in one soup and an ant in the other.

We called over the waitress and her face never flickered. She just got out a spoon and whipped both the fly and ant into a spare saucer and walked away without a word.

The most difficult things I had to sell were . . . let's call them Venus shampoo and Gleama-Dent.

My firm, being an American company, went out of their way to be spectacular at the official launch, even to the salesmen. Venus was a bright emerald green colour and the theme of the launch was: Think Emerald. There were Irish colleens, shamrock and even the champagne was dyed green. You could see which greedy pigs had been at the champagne because afterwards all the top executives were walking around with big green lips and tongues.

Gleama-Dent was a new product for false teeth.

Only a few months before our launch there was another similar new product from a competitor: Denti-Shine. This had flopped badly and every time we walked into a shop we would be faced with a huge mountain of Denti-Shine in the corner and your heart would sink. The shopkeeper would point and say: 'See that lot!' And *then* you would have to try and sell him another great mountain of Gleama-Dent.

The only people to buy it were the West Indians in West Bromwich and Balsall Heath. They had an incredible brand loyalty which they had brought over from the West Indies, and once they knew Gleama-Dent was made by my firm that was it. Virtually every salesman on the force was lugging crates of Gleama-Dent around these tiny shops in West Bromwich.

Who ever really wants to see a salesman?

A friend of mine applied for a job which read:

Are you selling? Are you confident? Do you want to get

ahead in this world? Do you want to earn £5000 a year for only five hours' work a week? Minimum qualifications needed. Smart appearance essential. Apply 5a, Paradise Street between 5 and 7 p.m.

He went on this course and they brainwashed him for three days. It was basically a vacuum cleaner which you could buy for fifteen quid, but he'd sell it you for forty. He had emerged a different person: someone who was going to conquer the world. Incredible aggression and confidence. They had convinced him that just about everyone in Britain wanted one of these cleaners. The first three house calls he made he sold three cleaners.

At the next house the door was opened by a very large Irishman, who after failing to be impressed by my friend's newly-acquired aggression, tried to insert the vacuum cleaner up a very delicate orifice. He was ruined in the space of three minutes!

He was like a lamb after that.

I'm probably a salesman's nightmare. I'm always sympathetic, because I know how frustrating the job is, but I am never caught as I learned all the tricks.

Someone pretending to be from the education authority once tried to sell a set of encyclopedias to me – and our daughter Lucy was only six months old.

'But she'll grow in to them,' he was saying. 'Just give her a chance.'

Roy Wood, salesmen's dream

Roy Wood would have been a different matter. Roy, who used to be with the pop groups The Move and Wizzard, is a salesman's dream. He always had friends who knew someone who sold bargains. . . .

He once bought a beautiful dog which looked straight from a Dulux paint advert. The whole of The Move went round to see it and thought: Thank Christ he's actually bought something right. Bev, who was the band's drummer at the time, starts to call him: 'Shep, Shep, here Shep.' And the dog was not taking a blind bit of notice. He spent the next hour creeping up on this dog and balling in his ear: 'Shep! Shep!' All the dog did was look out of the window at passing cars.

Bev says to Roy: 'Look, I think you might have a deaf dog here.'

'Deaf?' says Roy. 'Don't be ridiculous. He's only a puppy. He can't understand a word you're saying.'

Roy only believed it after a test The Move made. When the dog was asleep in front of the fire the whole group got tin cans and spoons and anything that would make a noise, crept up on it and when Bev yelled: 'Now!' they all started banging and screaming and making a God-Almighty row. Nothing.

Then they had another go, clashing and shouting right in his ears. Even one of the neighbours from across the street wandered over to see what was going on. Still nothing. Shep slept blissfully on, snoring away, with The Move setting up a constant barrage of noise louder than any rock concert.

Roy finally accepted that the dog just might be deaf and took him back. For once in his life he failed to be convinced by the salesman that there was nothing wrong and demanded a replacement. The guy finally gave in and handed Roy another dog.

It went lame after three days.

Roy always thought that everyone was his best friend. He actually managed to buy a brand new house which was haunted. It cost him £7000 at a time when the average priced detached house was £2500. Astronomical! And it hadn't even got central heating. So he had to get someone to put in a heating system and somehow managed to find an engineer who completed the job with no less than fourteen air locks. Roy had a choice: either move out or be haunted to death – the house would have fallen down anyway with the juddering from the central heating.

Biffer the dog

Mind you, when it comes to dogs anything can happen. I bought Biffer as a guard dog. He's a labrador who will do anything for a fuss. He will growl, bark and look ferocious. But you've only got to pat him on his head and he will roll over on his back and show you where the money is.

The only time I've seen him really roused was one night when all his hackles were raised and he was tense and snarling. I thought there must be at least a troupe of rapists in the garden, so I dashed out with a piece of iron piping in my hand. He paced twenty yards, dribbling and snarling across the back lawn – and came to a halt in front of the watering can. He leapt on top of it and ravaged it before I had time to stop him. To this day it's the only thing he will attack along with other male dogs.

If a pack of male dogs armed with watering cans tried to rob this house he would respond. But humans – no. He's not too keen on people who make essential deliveries, either. The postman, milkman or paper boy. But if someone wanted to steal the family silver – great!

He has this terrible habit of running away. After a time I found out where he was going: he lopes off down the towpath of the canal at the back of our house, runs along for three bridges and then walks in to the village of Knowle. There's a fish and chip shop where he sits outside and allows people to feed him.

I was always having to go out at all hours to pick him up in the car, so I decided to put a stop to it. If he went missing I would scramble into my car, drive for a mile and a half up the Warwick Road and stop at the canal bridge. There's a restaurant near this bridge and I would park my car there, dash out, down the towpath and hide behind the bushes to wait for Biffer.

When he came into sight I would leap out, usually with my right shoe in my hand.

All the diners in the restaurant have grown used to this. They see Carrott arrive in his car, park it and hide. This apparently innocent dog comes loping along the path by the canal only to be attacked by me with a shoe. I always shout: 'In your box – now.'

His 'box' is back at the house. He never twigs the fact that I'm not hard on his heels chasing him down the canal, so he turns tail and runs back. I get my shoe back on, I'm across the bridge, into the car and arrive in the house before he does. So when Biffer comes through the door I can see him thinking: 'How the hell has he got back here before me?'

This ritual has been going on for five years now. Supposedly laugh-a-minute Carrott turning up with a face like thunder to beat an apparently lovable, friendly dog. It's a wonder I haven't been arrested.

Labradors are particularly greedy dogs and Biffer is greedier than any of them. It's made him so strong. I used to tie him to a water pump with a huge concrete block at the bottom. But one day I had a phone call from the police saying: 'I've just seen your dog dragging a water pump and a concrete block down the A41.' I end up driving out to pick up Biffer *and* the concrete block, which I could hardly lift.

Two years ago we decided to mate him. A friend brought a female dog around to our house and Biffer went bonkers. And the bitch wanted to know. You've heard the joke about two people riding a tandem and an alsatian running out and throwing a bucket of water over them.... Up to that point I hadn't realized that two dogs could become locked while they're copulating. Friends and neighbours had come round for a drink and were all watching these two dogs through the windows, and ended up filing out to give their own personal instructions of how to prise them apart. I don't know about Biffer, but there were tears in *my* eyes. Eventually, nature took its own course.

Since then, he's been the greediest, most unloyal, worst guard dog *and* the randiest in the neighbourhood....

My left leg, which I found out recently is half an inch shorter than the right, is *always* being raped by dogs.

When I would talk to my prospective in-laws I always used to try and feign innocence about what their dog was doing to me. It is absolutely impossible to sip tea, make polite conversation and gently push off the dog when he's ardently trying to rape your left leg. Everyone would pretend not to notice.

I started going out with Hazel, my wife, when she was only seventeen and I was twenty-four. She was still at school and I didn't want to give the impression to her parents that I was an aware twenty-four year-old being turned on by a schoolgirl. But every time I arrived to take her out it would be the same. I would be there trying to discuss my job prospects, mortgages and house prices while their dog was crawling up my left leg.

Arthur the hamster

We never had pets at home with my parents.

We had the occasional cat, but we were on a main road and it would be run over after about three days. In our road anything living that did not have human intelligence would be dead within a week.

So we would be plagued by mice, because no cat lived long enough to catch them. I remember coming home about one o'clock in the morning once and I heard this scratching coming from a cardboard box. Mice! I got hold of a broomhandle, turned the light on and sneaked up on it. I was just about to hammer the crap out of it when I realized I was looking at a hamster.

I woke my mother and said: 'There's a hamster downstairs in a box.'

'I know,' she says. 'That's Arthur.'

'Where's he from?'

'Your brother has brought him home.'

My brother was twenty-eight at the time. He was unmarried and had decided on a hamster instead.

For one week all is well. Everyone makes a fuss of the hamster and he's running around, lying on his back to be tickled and everything's fine. Then, gradually, we start to notice this smell. The hamster, according to my mum, has been pissing in the grate.

'He'll have to go,' she said, 'because he's a little bleeder.'

My mum had the grate out, put Dettol down and anything else that would kill smells. But it made no difference. Then I happened to touch one of the plugs near an electric fire. It was red hot. Dad was an electrician yet we probably had the worst wiring in the world. You had to hold the TV aerial in with a couple of matchsticks. Typical electrician's house – turn the telly on and you'd boil a kettle.

So the smell had been burning plastic and Arthur had won a reprieve.

Then, a few days later, we got up and found that 'Arthur' had given birth to twelve children. Bloody little hamsters everywhere. My mum finally went bonkers.

Even worse, after a short time they started copulating together. Now this, to my mother, was pornography. It was much worse than laying your girlfriend in the front room.

So she got hold of biscuit tins, cardboard boxes, jam-jars – and had them separated in twos. Every ten minutes she would get up to see whether they were at it. It was the only way she could find out which were male and female. You can never tell with hamsters.

She spent the whole night until three in the morning trying to sex these little animals: 'You leave him alone! You dirty little basket! Get off her!'

My brother had bought 'Arthur' every conceivable toy: wheels to turn round; things to play with; even a Hamster Palace. But he'd lost interest after about a week. He'd got bored because it hadn't been run over like the cats.

In the end my mother got all the males together and all the females together. But they would leap out of each other's little boxes and start all over again. They had to go – and so did Arthur.

Still, they all left my leg alone. . . .

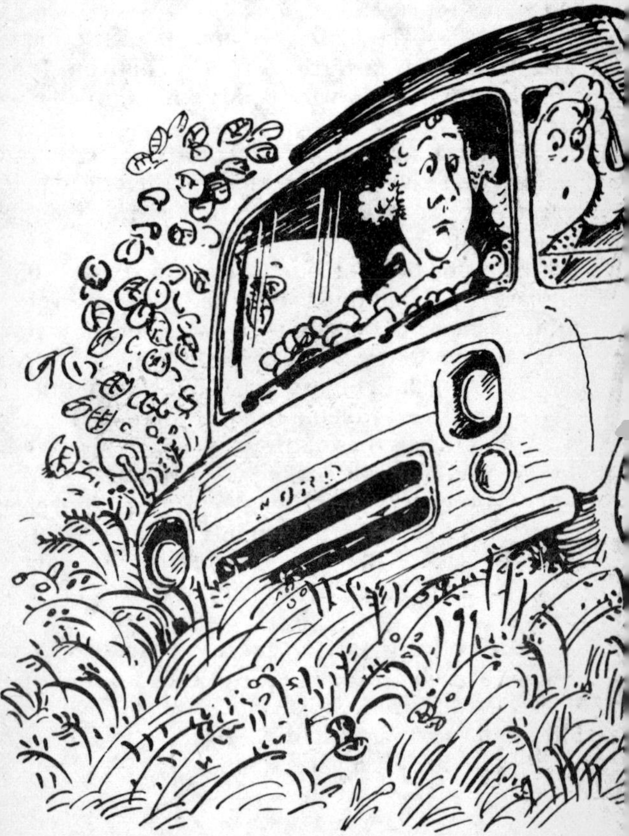

4 The Road to Redditch

Caught-ing

To all mothers I was like a shiftless layabout who would do their daughters no good at all. The George Mason's grocery delivery van didn't help.

I was working as a George Mason's delivery boy because they couldn't get anybody else. And I used to ask if I could take the van home so I could make a start early the next day. It was a two-ton van with 'George Mason' written in huge lettering on the side.

When I first met Hazel I picked her up in the van. Her mother was singularly unimpressed. They had spent a lifetime of grafting and paying out a fortune on her education. To see their daughter stepping into a van on a date must have been depressing for them.

We had only been going a couple of miles along a country lane when a car came the other way. I went to one side to avoid it and sank the delivery van into a ditch. Hazel was forty-five degrees, hanging on to the dashboard. I had to do something faintly impressive, so I slid out and went to a nearby farmer to get him to tow us.

If there was anything worse than seeing their daughter going *out* in this van, it must have been the sight of her returning, three hours later, pale-faced and trembling, after spending the evening slouched in a seat only a couple of feet above a muddy ditch while a tractor heaved the van from side to side.

She was also smelling of bacon.

Then there was a date with a girl called Rosalind. She was a doctor.

Her mother didn't like me at all. She thought I'd never make anything of myself – and turning up in a George Mason's van confirmed her views. Her doctor daughter getting into this van to go to a Chinese restaurant! I parked the van near the Chinese, which was quite close to the George Mason's shop in Solihull.

When we came out two hours later after an entirely unexceptional meal there was no van.

I was frantic. And she was none too pleased having to get the bus home. The police were on the case for hours before announcing: 'We've found the van.'

'Where?'

'At the back of George Mason's.'

What had happened was the manager was working late, had come out of the shop around eight, had seen the van and had used a set of spare keys to drive it round to the back of the shop.

The next day he spent most of the time telling me off: 'The van shouldn't be out. It should be here. You mustn't take the van.' And I was grounded.

I think the mothers of Solihull felt much happier after that.

Bognor to The Boggery

So I applied to work in Butlin's Holiday Camp. I thought I'd have the time of my life with all those Swedish students. I couldn't be a Redcoat because you had to be a professional entertainer. I'd have gone as a Dufflecoat – anything, in fact. And that's what I ended up doing – anything. It was called a kitchen porter and I was based in Bognor Regis.

I worked from seven in the morning until half past four, six days a week, with an hour's break a day. Shifting 56lb blocks of frozen meat and supplying the kitchens. I learned a lot about boredom: when the mind has nothing to think about it conceives things that are not really there. I got into arguments about who had lifted more boxes. The highlight of a working week was to go over the road to a local boozer where they sold scrumpy at one shilling and threepence a pint and get paralytic.

There was this entertainer at the camp doing the most obscene act I've ever seen outside a stag night. He did a routine about Big Dick getting between Open Legs in a horse race – about as subtle as a bucket of lard. And that used to be the most popular request from the audience!

I started a folk club for some of the staff just as a way of trying to relieve some of the boredom. It lasted almost as long as I did at Butlin's in Bognor; three months.

My home address at the time was *Shaft*more Lane, A*cocks* Green – like a home for a professional rapist. From there I started my first folk club proper at Acocks Green Conservative Club and soon afterwards opened The Boggery in Solihull.

I cringe now when I think what I used to do at that club. I only knew two songs. At the start of the evening I would ask the audience: 'Do you want number one or number two?' Number one was 'Wild Rover' and number two was 'Gypsy Rover'. Or there was 'Wild Gypsy Rover', 'Rover, Rover' or a combination of anything to get me through those first twenty minutes. Things don't change. . . .

I started a folk agency to get work for myself and others and decided to call it 'Fingimigig Agency', meaning 'Find-me-a-gig' – but no one understood it. One day I had to place an advert in the *Birmingham Evening Mail* to advertise The Boggery Folk Club. I got a girl on telephone ads who I hadn't dealt with before.

'Go ahead,' she says.

'The Boggery Folk Club. . .'

'Pardon?'

'B-o-g-g-e-r-y.'

'Yees.'

'Lug Trout Lane. . .'

'What?'

'L-u-g T-r-o-u-t. . .'

'Yees.'

'Presents, the Pigsty Hill Light Orchestra. . .'

'The Pig what?'

'P-i-g-s-t-y.'

'Yees. . .'

'And Jasper Carrott. . .'

'Who?'

'C-a-r-r-o-t-t.'

'Yees. . .'

Then I give her the date and time.

53

'Where do I send this bill?' she asks.

'It's the Fingimigig Agency... F-i-n-g...'

'Oooh!' she shrieks. 'I know it's you, Kevin. I'll see you at eight o'clock tonight as usual. Ta-ra!'

My partner in Fingimigig was John Starkey, now my personal manager and right-hand man. We have very similar voices on the phone; even our wives can't tell us apart. It was always useful for me to pose as John to tell people how fantastic Jasper Carrott was. It was equally useful for him to pose as me when his creditors were coming through.

Scunthorpe Baths

I suppose it was the hit single 'Funky Moped' and Scunthorpe Baths which changed all that.

I was number five in the charts with 'Funky Moped' and suddenly John was offered six hundred quid for me to play at Scunthorpe Baths. For one night! It was more then I'd earned in the last six months.

We were there in plenty of time. The dressing room was the boiler-room underneath the Baths. We'd been sitting waiting for about half an hour when this bloke dashes in: 'Jasper Carrott?'

'Yep.'

'Great! Where's the equipment?'

'Well, we'd hoped to use yours.'

'How many of you are there?'

'Just me.'

'On your own?'

'Yep.'

'Well . . . er, what do you do?'

'I'm a comic.'

'What – like Bernard Manning?'

'No. Nothing like that.'

'What then?'

'A folk-singing comic.'

Silence.

This Bath's manager, whose concession to Saturday night was to wear a coloured tie with his grey suit, had just realized he had made one big bloomer. He'd got

1200 kids on the boards in those Baths waiting to hear a pop group. The week before they'd had 'Kenny'; the week before that 'Slik' – all those teeny-bopper groups around the time of the Bay City Rollers.

He went back upstairs and returned, ashen-white: 'The disc jockey's got a microphone,' he says. 'You'll have to use that.'

He was panicking – and so was I.

I went upstairs to have a look and there's a packed hall with kids aged thirteen to seventeen. I thought: 'You can either run, or do something and pick up six hundred quid.'

The stage was exactly three inches high with about fifty of the 1200 packed tightly around it. So I had to walk through them all with my guitar to get on this 'stage' and be faced with fifty blank expressions about four inches from the end of my nose. I could almost hear them thinking: 'Gink. We've got a gink. It's another gink. Seventy-five pence for this Scunthorpe Baths rip-off.'

The rest of them were hanging from the balcony or were in the bar. At that point I was announced. The expressions grew blanker. The only thing I could do was to go back in my mind to the early songs of The Boggery Folk Club, so I started singing 'Coming Round the Mountain', 'Wild Rover' and 'Chastity Belt'. Anything, in fact, to fill in time. I sang 'Hava Nagila' three times!

In the end I'd got about 400 kids around the 'stage' and they were going bonkers. Don't ask me why. I hadn't got a clue. I went off to this storm of applause and I got as far as the side of the hall. I thought: Christ, they're asking for a bloody encore.

Meanwhile, John Starkey, who had been hopping around praying for a miracle, had got as far as the Bath manager's office. The manager had been counting out the fivers very slowly – especially when he heard the opening of 'Hava Nagila' for the third time.

As soon as he finished, Starkey snatched it from him, ran down the stairs and got the car ready.

He came back into the Baths just in time to see me making my way from the stage and he screamed in my ear: 'I've got the money.'

'Great!' I shouted. 'Let's get the hell out of here.'

I didn't know what they'd seen in it all. For fifty minutes I'd been in a blind panic.

We left 400 screaming kids, the manager shouting for an encore and us screeching down the road in the car, counting the money. . . .

John Starkey, the collector

Ever since I've known John Starkey he's always been a collector.

He is totally non-sporting. Mention jogging and he'll break into a sweat. When he was a kid he would collect frogs, moths, bats, newts – anything that moved, flew or swam. He's really into First and Second World War history: cars, planes, bikes, tanks, ships and anti-aircraft missiles. He has this immense knowledge that is absolutely useless.

His poor wife! His entire house is littered with Woolworth plane kits. You go to his office and see great planes hanging down from the ceiling that he's not quite finished. His knowledge is fantastic. He knows everyone who took part in the First World War. He knows the size of boots, colour of uniforms, names – anything.

When you're on tour with him he can be a real pain. You're driving down the motorway and he suddenly shouts: *'My God!!'* You think you're at least going into the back of a truck ... or one of the motorway service stations is falling in on you. And he's seen a Ferrari coming up the other way: 'A 308 GT4 with a V8-2926 engine! Blimey! They only made about eight of those!'

He buys all the magazines like *War* and army manuals. Anything mechanical he's in to. But he wouldn't know if he's got a flat battery in his car. He wouldn't have a clue. He would know who made the battery and what type it was – but he wouldn't know how it worked. The biggest pain of all is to get him with someone else who knows all about that rubbish. Then it's like listening to a foreign language. They just talk in numbers and figures.

He buys anything. Now he's got a bit more money he upgrades it. From buying Woolworth sets he now goes for a Jaguar XK-120, a Jaguar E-Type and a Daimler. His missus has a Fiat-190. Rather than buy toy models he now gets the real thing. I'm expecting a Chieftan tank in his front garden at any time.

We did a gig in Southend once and right opposite was a plane museum. I never saw him. He actually went there when it was closed and persuaded the guy in charge to open it up. He knew more about what he'd got than the museum curator. The guy offered him a job.

His ambition is to own a Ferrari. There are very few people who can match his knowledge. You'd have to be Montgomery to know more about the Second World War. He was born in 1944, missed the war and has regretted the fact all his life. He's got every model plane Woolworth has ever sold – and a lot more besides. He kept all his train sets from being a kid.

John was always the kid on the railway bridge, in airport lounges, on street corners taking notes of British Road Transport numbers and in bus depots, forever wandering round with a book and pencil in his hand.

VAT-man

Of course, the trouble with being both self-employed and earning anything more than the poverty level is the dreaded VAT-man.

A cold shiver ran down my pocket when he wanted to see me. Now, my books and footballers' autographs have one thing in common: they are complete gibberish except to the person who writes them.

And the receipts! He'd want to see the receipts. I'd stuffed all mine carefully into a cardboard box the telly came in – except that I can't find the cardboard box.

'Hazel, where's that box the new telly came in?'

'It's in the kid's playroom. They're using it to play war.'

Some of the receipts had been used as swabs for their hospital game; most had a deposit of food smeared on them; the rest had been eaten.

I gathered up the remains of the receipts and put them into official-looking files I'd bought secondhand from an undertaker.

I sat in a cold sweat awaiting the VAT-man's arrival. As he came through the front door he was most careful to avoid treading on my hands! He helped me up and I ushered him into the lounge where he drank several cups of tea and examined the books. To my great surprise, he could actually understand them.

He moved quickly, checked the receipts, asked for a cloth to wipe the marmite off his hands and proclaimed everything was fine and he must be away to his next call.

I couldn't believe it. I started garbling on about what a wonderful job he was doing and he must come again. He smiled, stepped over me and bid farewell. . . .

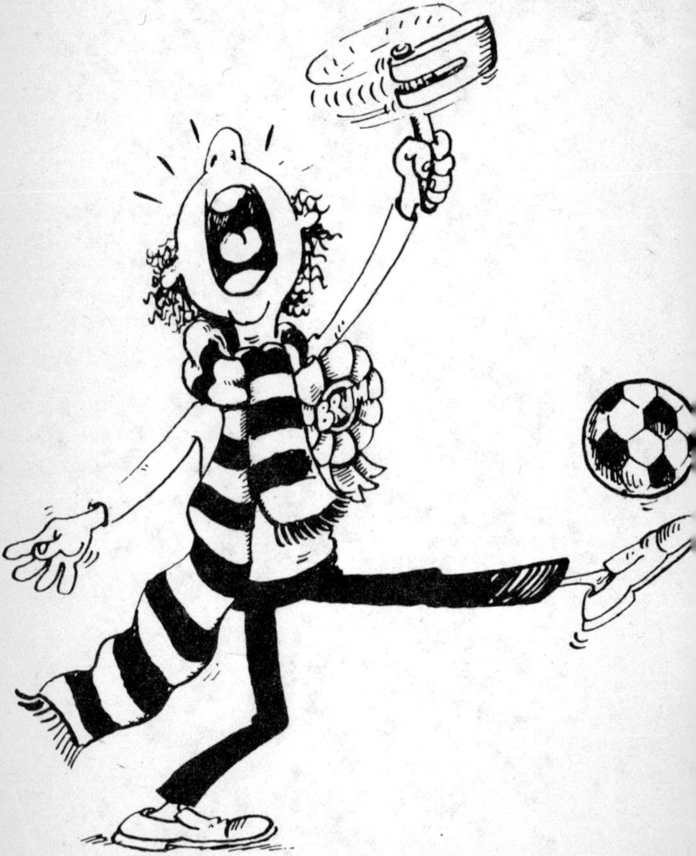

5 Soccer Groupie

Sunday football

They say there are two million people in this country who play soccer – the vast majority of them on Sunday morning. At ten o'clock groups of red-eyed men are waiting around pub car parks. They look as if they've just turned out of the pub, huddled together for warmth or kicking a tin can around rather discontentedly.

Then a convoy of near-MOT failures come up, with broken wings and rotten undersides, and this group of men pile into the cars.

They arrive at parks on the edge of towns and cities and meet the man with the power of life: the Park Keeper. He has the key to the dressing room. You get a chit from the Football League to say that you've got a pitch booked for that morning. You present that chit to the 'parkie'. There could be twenty-four guys waiting for one bloke – the one with the chit for the dressing room. That parkie won't let you near the place until he sees it. It's his one moment of power every Sunday morning and he wields it.

The dressing room is like a chicken run, all wire and thin wood, with only ten hooks and ten seats for eleven players. The parks themselves seem to have twenty-four pitches but the 'parkie' is never around to tell you which pitch is which. You can be halfway through a game before you find that you're playing the wrong team.

Then after the game there's twenty-four pitches and twenty-two blokes on each pitch for six jets in the showers. And there's always one slither of soap, hanging on a piece of string, often round someone's neck. And wherever you play there are only two types of pitches: one is like the north face of the Eiger – a clamp-on job and you have to throw ropes down to haul your team-mates up. The other is the type where you toss up to decide who defends the shallow end.

You play on land that no one wants, in games that no one wants to watch, at times when every sane man is either in bed or down the pub, with half the players still recovering from last night's hangover.

But then that's the joy of Sunday soccer. And I'd never miss it.

To me, soccer is more than just a game. I've been crazy about it since 1955 when I first went to watch Birmingham City in their promotion year from the Second Division. And among the people I most admire are top-class professional footballers.

I did a Professional Footballers Association after-dinner speech one year and met a lot of players. Malcolm MacDonald, who was then playing for Newcastle United, was trying to organize a testimonial game for Frank Clarke who had left United after thirteen years' service. The club's reward had been a free transfer.

Malcolm wanted me to do a concert in Newcastle City Hall to raise some money towards the testimonial. I arrived in the morning to train with the team and then Malcolm, myself and the reserve centre-forward went for lunch. The reserve was called Paul Cannell – a name I hadn't heard before. I picked up on it right away: 'Porkinell' was how it was pronounced, if you said it very fast. I was highly delighted with this find and was going round saying: 'What the Porkinell's going on round here, then?'

We went into a city restaurant about noon and it was completely empty. Malcolm said: 'A table for three, please.'

The waitress said: 'Hang on. I'll see if we've got any room.' In a totally empty restaurant! We all started to laugh and, when she returned and said: 'If you go to the bar I'll see whether I can fit you in', it cracked us up completely. From then on it was a jokey afternoon with a few drinks and a few stories flying around. We didn't leave the place until about four o'clock.

I had bought this Daimler car a couple of days before and we all piled into it. I had a chauffeur's hat, put it on and it was silly devils' time, pressing my face onto the windscreen, with Paul Cannell shouting *'Porkinell'* out of the window. Malcolm was slumped in the back and it was all getting out of hand.

Eventually the inevitable happened. A policeman waved us down. I turned to press the electric window so I could lean out and talk to him. But I pressed the back one by mistake. So this copper sticks his head through the back window and suddenly notices Malcolm.

'Wor, Malcolm!' he says. 'Wor . . . I think you're fantastic. Every Saturday, Malcolm, I see you knocking them in. Wor . . . wor, it's great to see you.'

He'd got his notebook out to book me and instead he thrusts it into Malcolm's face: 'I've got these three brothers, Malcolm, and they think you're magic . . . Wor, when I tell them I've seen ya, lad.' He'd got Malcolm signing autographs in his police book.

The instant he finished signing I'd got the window rolled up and the car moving again: 'Wor, Malcolm, see you on Saturday, lad,' he was shouting.

Malcolm was like a god in Newcastle.

It was fascinating to watch people's faces when they saw him. St James's Park, the home ground of Newcastle United, is right on the outskirts of the city centre. Anywhere in the city centre you can see St

James's Park's floodlights. It's only a couple of minutes walk.

I kept on stopping the car, with my silly hat on sideways, to ask people where St James's Park was. They'd hardly take any notice until they saw Malcolm. . . .

'Wor! Worrr! It's Malcolm . . . WOR! Sign this bus ticket, Malcolm . . . WORRR!'

They would have a long conversation with Malcolm MacDonald – then tell him where St James's Park was.

That's the power of soccer.

"'ello Tone, 'arry 'ere"

There's a guy called Tony Butler, sports presenter on BRMB, the Birmingham radio station. He's so bad he's brilliant. Football predictions? He's one hundred per cent wrong!

Football teams have told me that they sit in front of the set at twenty to three on a Saturday afternoon, waiting for the Butler Prediction. If he predicts them to win they don't bother to get changed – they just go home.

On a Saturday he does a phone-in show two o'clock to seven o'clock in the evening, and they've had to introduce a four-second delay on transmissions. He's a fairly controversial character and has a go at everybody. People tend to phone up and disagree with him. The engineer has got four seconds to hit that delay button and a jingle goes out instead, just in time to get the obscenities out.

The people who phone him are priceless, particularly after the games on a Saturday: "'ello, Tone. What about the Villa then, eh?'

'Yeah. What about them?'

'Thanks, Tone.'

Or: "'ello, Tone, I was down St Andrews today and they were magic. Keith Birchin hit this one ball and if it had gone in the net it would 'ave bin a goal!'

He does competitions as well like: 'This competition is for two free tickets for last year's Cup Final.

What are Andy Gray's initials?' Then you get a call: "ello, Tone. Is it 1973?'

'Yeah, you've won, you're the nearest, right.'

(BRMB also do a special programme for the Asian community. It had been on six months before they realized that the presenter was advertising his grocery shop.)

But the Butler classic?

It was a couple of seasons ago and West Bromwich Albion were going hard for promotion to the First Division. Everyone in Birmingham *knew* they were going to go up – because Butler had predicted they would go down to the Third. There's no way they're going to miss promotion now, but they have to go through the formality of playing the games.

It came towards the end of the season and West Bromwich Albion had to go to Oldham Athletic – and if they beat Oldham they would go up to the First Division. Now this is a big day for BRMB, Butler and all the Albion fans. So Butler gets one of his henchmen to go up to Oldham for the game. God knows where he gets them from. I think he pops out into Aston Road and says: 'Hey, you – want to go to Oldham?'

So he sends this bloke up to Oldham with the name of Harry Trifiley. He comes on the air with reports like: 'This is 'arry Trifiley, BRMB Radio, and the Albion are playing very well. Now back to you, Tone.' Halfway through the second half the Albion score: 'This is 'arry Trifiley, BRMB Radio and the Albion have scored . . . the Albion have scored. It's a forty-yard header from Tony Brown who hits it with his foot and, anyway, if the Albion can hold on to this goal and Oldham don't score I think they'll win. Back to you, Tone.'

At the end of the game the Albion win and are back in the First Division, so Tony Butler has to do something special. He gets hold of Trifiley on the phone off the air and bawls: "'arry. Go and get one of the Albion players and we'll do an interview with him on the air. All right?'

'Righto.'

'Right! On your bike. Okay?'

Harry comes back and says: 'Tone, I've got John Osborne here, the Albion goalkeeper, and he's going to do an interview with us. All right?'

'Stick with him, 'arry. We're gonna have a commercial break and I'll announce it after that.'

So he plays a commercial break and comes in after the adverts and says: 'What a fantastic day this is for West Bromwich Albion and BRMB. The Albion have smashed Oldham one-nil and hammered their way into the First Division like what I predicted — well, almost — and as it's a special day for Albion fans and BRMB, our Man-at-the-Match 'arry Trifiley is talking to none other than the Albion goalkeeper John Osborne. Come in 'arry...'arry?...'arry!...*arry!*'

"ello, Tone...Tone, he's pissed off.'

Villa Parkers

I get around to visiting quite a few grounds, and every football club has someone who will try and stop you getting into their private car park.

Aston Villa is the worst.

They have two men that *nothing* can get past.

I've always said that Birmingham City should sign them and put them in the back four.

I was a VIP guest of an executive sponsor at Villa Park. I'd got every ticket, pass and form that was going and I turned up to present them at the car park.

'Hello,' said I. 'I'm Jasper Carrott and I'm guest at Fred Copson's box, the executive sponsor.'

His expression didn't change: 'You got a car park pass?'

'No. But I've got these executive sponsor tickets which allow me anywhere in the ground. I think I could even kick off.'

'I know who you are,' says he. 'But you can't come in because you haven't got a pass.'

'But the VIP guest is expecting me. . .'

'I don't care. A couple of minutes ago I even turned away a cripple. Didn't I, Joe?'

He turns to his mate.

'Yeh, he did, yeh, a cripple he was . . . in one of them long wheelchair things.'

'He couldn't come in, see. Didn't have a pass.'

'We had to push him back out in the middle of the road, you know. Didn't have a reverse gear.'

'He didn't have to get out of his wheelchair, though, did he, Joe? We did it for him. . . .'

Motor spares man

I think car park attendants go into that job because they can cause most pain to the public.

The blokes who sell motor spares are even worse. They are all well-balanced with a chip on each shoulder, all wear white coats, all have huge reams of paper in front of them and will always keep you waiting while they study these sheets.

You might have been queueing for half an hour and finally get through to one of them and ask for what you want. Then he will raise a silent hand and point to the man next to him, dealing with another long queue of people, and you'll have to start all over again.

Then some snotty-nosed kid comes in covered in oil, like a walking grease-nipple, and asks: 'Four by two Evans, I type of pipe, Ems 14 TR 606 Y' and suddenly the man in the white coat leaps into action.

The grease-nipple will be out inside a minute with a big box and the white coat just turns to the unbelieving queue and announces: 'Trade!'

I went in for a clip on a Ford Anglia once and when I managed to get in front of the queue – and white-coat acknowledged me – I said: 'I want a clip for a Ford Anglia...'

'What sort of Anglia? There are thousands of Anglias.'

'Well, it's just a...'

'Mark One or Two?'
"Er, 1963.'
'Aaah! *Pre*-Mark One.'

They go out and return with a tiny clip, spend ten minutes filling out a massive form and then charge about £3.50. By that time you're too tired to argue at the price or anything else.

On that huge sheet of paper I'm sure there are spaces for your age, where you live and references. Go into a spares shop for a new ashtray and you will probably have to buy a new car door!

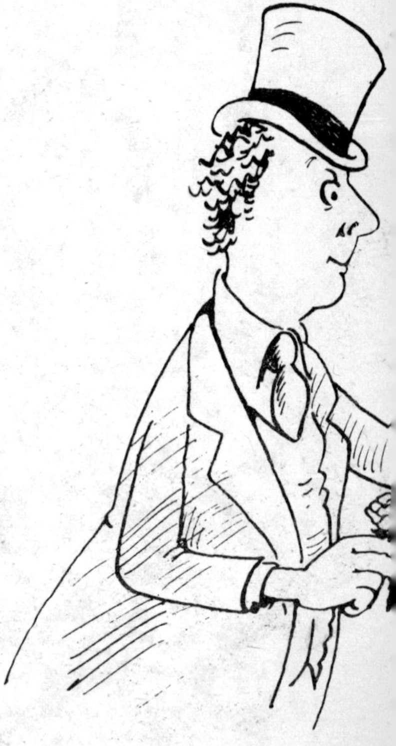

6 The Wedding

I was recently asked to be an usher at a wedding in Bickenhill Church: a very old church in a picturesque little village. A very flash place to get married and the groom wanted a top hat and tails affair, which meant me going to Moss Bros.

(I did a very foolish thing by getting measured for the suit and hat, then having my hair cut. The hat rested neatly on top of my ears.)

They had obviously spent an age planning this wedding. Everything was supposed to be perfectly organized. I was given the job of putting buttonholes on people.

Now the old part of the church was very small, but there had been a large new extension built with a better view of the altar. The groom told me: 'We have hundreds of relatives coming and they have to sit in the new extension. Make sure we get all the friends in the old part of the church.'

'How do I know which is which?'

'Ask them,' he says.

So as each couple or party enter the church I say: 'Friend or relative?' And while I was asking I was attempting to put buttonholes on women wearing frocks. They're looking at me suspiciously, thinking: 'He wants to fondle my breasts.' And I'm thinking: 'God, I hope I don't touch their breasts.' Now I don't know whether you're familiar with frocks, but they are big terylene flower jobs, with plenty of breasts showing, usually worn by women whose husbands are in demob suits.

I was there, like some sex maniac, grabbing hold of these women to stick red rose buttonholes in to their frocks. I'm trying to avoid touching their breasts, sticking the pins in my fingers and blood is pouring down the frocks.

After ten minutes of this I'm also packing the friends in at a rate of knots and there's hardly a relative in the place. There's this new section practically empty and dozens of friends packed into this tiny old corner of the church.

I was asking: 'Friends or relatives?'

'Friends.'

'You'll have to go over there.'

'Why can't we sit in all that space?

'Reserved for relatives.'

Couples were saying: 'We can't possibly sit in there!' And those already seated were saying: 'No, please. No more. Please.' There were people sitting who could hardly breathe. If they got down on their knees to pray there would be someone sitting in their seat.

I went to the groom and told him: 'There's absolutely no room up there – and the bride has just arrived.'

'Okay,' he says. 'Move them from the old part so they can sit in the new section and get a good view. All the relatives have obviously decided not to come.'

So these friends could spread out at last, gasping for air and loosening the buttons on their suits. I walk calmly back to the door to welcome the bride and I could not believe it. Behind the bride's car was about twenty or thirty cars all arriving in convoy. The frocks and demob suits were all piling out of these Rovers and A40s and I thought: 'God, no!'

I had to rush back to the friends and start pleading with them to go back to the seats in the old part. Nothing doing. There was no way they were going back to be suffocated. So I start dragging the friends into the old part, the choir is making its way down the aisle – stepping over wrestling bodies and bloodied frocks – breathless relatives are panting and hustling from the back and a flustered bride is being assured by the vicar that this is indeed her wedding day and not Armaggedon.

The bride's mother ends up at the back of the church and the person who's arranged the flowers gets a seat at the front. . . .

Afterwards the crowd is milling around in the car park asking exactly where the reception is.

I have no idea.

I sit in the car and wait for someone to go, so I can follow them. Nobody is moving. Then this one bloke starts off and he looks confident so I follow him. Within half a second there is a screeching of tyres and a whole convoy is behind me, bumper to bumper.

The bloke goes about three miles and then turns left into his drive. I turn left into his drive. About forty other cars behind me turn left into his drive.

We all reverse out again – but I'm still in front of the pack. So I carry on as far as Stonebridge Island near Coventry and I do a complete circuit to see if there's any sign of wedding cars disappearing along any of the exits. As I go around for the first time the last of the cars following *me* emerges from the road on to the island. We follow each other's tails for a full five minutes before anyone has enough courage to take the lead.

When we all finally got to the reception the speeches had already started.

It was announced that 'Uncle George' was about to give us a speech. Now I didn't know Uncle George, but as the father of the bride made the announcement I could hear the murmurings and grumbles and it's obvious that Uncle George is a bit of a pain.

He puts a briefcase on a table at the back of the room and everyone has to turn around to look at Uncle George. He opens the case, takes out sheafs of paper which look as if he's preparing for a lecture rather than a speech and said: 'It gives me great pleasure...'

As he does so the table collapses, with crockery, wine, food, cheese, biscuits, coffee, tumbling over everybody. Mayhem! Uncle George is looking crestfallen and a voice calls out in the chaos: 'I think you'd better forget it this time, George....'

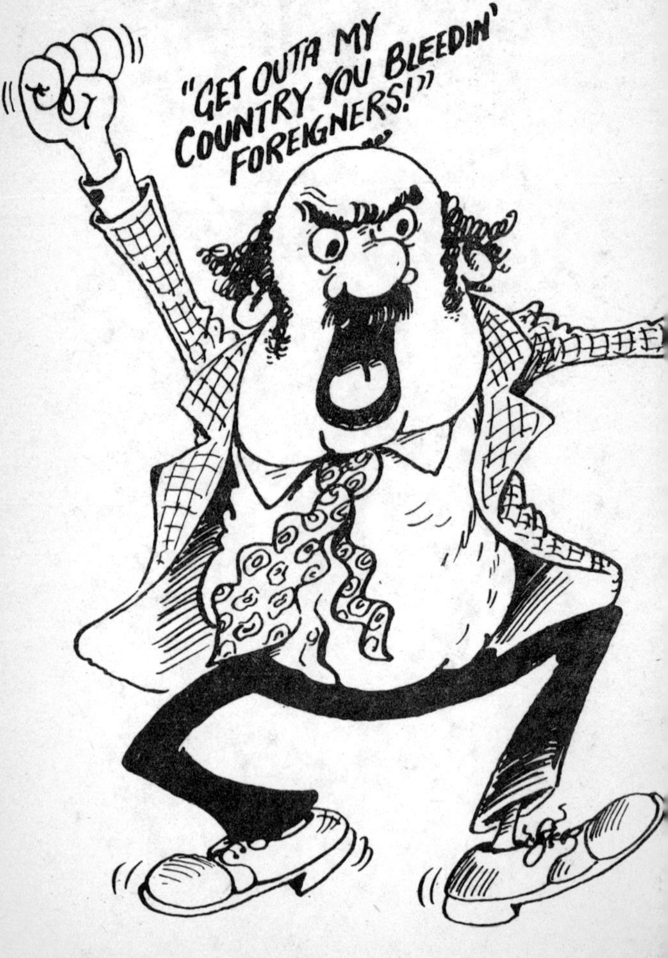
"GET OUTA MY
COUNTRY YOU BLEEDIN'
FOREIGNERS!"

7 Foreigners and Other Problems

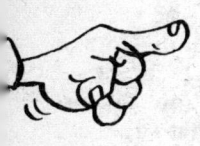

The Italian job

Much more relaxing and soothing on the nerves are Foreign Trips. At least, they are usually. But the Italy-England World Cup qualifying game in Rome was a little different.

I joined a party of Midlanders which included a very well-known Italian restaurant owner from Birmingham called Lorenzo. For years he had taken all the stick from the regular customers – he was called the Brummie Mafia, they criticized his Italian cooking and spoke to him in a falsa-Italian-accent.

As the plane was coming in to land at Rome airport we're all sitting strapped into our seats, as it's always a tense moment when any aircraft touches down. The second the wheels connected with the runway, Lorenzo leapt out of his seat, stormed to the front of the plane, pointed at all of us sitting dumbly watching him and yelled: 'Get outa my country you bleedin' foreigners!'

We arrived, all in a very boozed state from the plane, at the Rome Hilton. I was to share a room with one of the British reporters, called Martin, but we hardly had time to check in properly. The Italians, who are soccer crazy, were already trying to storm the stadium, so we thought we'd all better get down there fast. We got through all five security checks around the stadium and tumbled into the bar – only to find it completely empty. We couldn't believe it and got stuck into a few more drinks. But when we came to go to our seats we discovered why the bar had been deserted.

There must have been four Italians to every seat. Ticket numbers? Forget it. They didn't mean a thing. The police were spraying tear gas around the place like air freshener. I didn't see the first twenty minutes of the game because my eyes were filled with water.

Then there was poor Billy Wright.... The ex-England captain, who was one of our party, was jammed in by wild Italians as he vainly looked for his seat. The man who won 105 caps gives up trying to watch the game, looks at those around him and starts telling this incredibly boring story about how Puskas scored one of the best goals of all time by pulling the ball back with his right foot and hitting it with his left all in one swift movement. A journalist at the time had said in his report: 'Wright was going into the tackle like a fire engine going to the wrong fire...' Billy was in his element, surrounded by all these people who hadn't heard his story. Especially as they had no way of escape. I could not believe that none of the Italians knew who he was. I kept telling them: 'Don't you know who he is? He's married to one of the Beverley Sisters.'

After the game, which England lost, Lorenzo is determined to cheer us up and takes us to a restaurant. I'm wearing my one and only suit – which is white – and one of the waiters takes one look and thinks I'm a member of the England team.

'Where you play?' he asks.

'Me, Greenhoff – I'm number four.'

This he accepted and we were instant celebrities.

I then started introducing the others. A fat, balding middle-aged businessman became 'Bobby Charlton, who's here for the day.' A tiny thin little guy was 'Les Cocker, the trainer.' I was carried away by it in the end – 'this George Best,' I said, pointing to a guy with long hair and a beard, 'and Pele is in a car round the corner, drunk.'

By three o'clock in the morning they'd begun to twig there was something wrong, particularly as professional footballers aren't supposed to drink wine by the gallon.

I returned to the hotel to find that the reporter, Martin, had got our room key. I thought: 'How the hell am I going to find him at this hour?'

A drunk, who I recognized as being a respectable barrister from Birmingham, was staggering down the corridor, so I asked him if he'd seen Martin: 'Room 511,' he slurred and crumpled in a heap at my feet.

By the time I'd reached the third floor I could *hear* room 511. Just like a radiation blast of noise. Martin was there, plus twelve blokes, including an Italian hairdresser who shall be nameless.

'Ah,' I gasped, 'great. Let's have the room key, Martin, I'm dying to go to bed.'

'Jasper! Come on. Have a drink.'

'No, thanks. I've been drinking all night.'

'Have just the one before you go to bed.'

'All I want is the key.'

'Name your drink first.'

'All right,' say I, 'can I have a beer?'

'Sorry, no beer. Whisky, wine, vodka, gin – no beer. Order the man a beer from room service!'

I sit on the bed, exasperated, and then notice for the first time there's a girl in the room. I'm thinking: 'I haven't seen a girl on this trip at all. What's she doing in here?' The girl is talking to the Italian.

After about fifteen minutes I'm getting really drowsy. There's still no sign of the beer – and all I want is the room key. I'm just about to ask for it again when the Italian comes up: 'Jasper – give me five pounds.'

'What?'

'Give-a-me-five-pound.'

'What for?'

'Donta you trust me?'

I'm too tired to argue and hand him a fiver. I vaguely notice he's walking around the room getting five pounds from everyone. I'm just about to ask for the key when the Italian suddenly shoves all £60 between the girl's breasts. She giggles and instantly starts taking her clothes off.

I say: 'Is this beer going to be long?'

But the bird has stripped down to her bra and pants and is walking across the room towards me. I put my hands up to protect myself, but all she does is pull down my zip and get my plonker out!

It's that sort of very embarrassing situation. I mean, what do you do? I didn't want to appear a spoilsport and not be one of the lads or anything, so I left it out. She walks around the room undoing zips. All the guys are in an alcoholic daze – most of them very wealthy and respectable – all standing with drinks in their hands and trousers around their ankles.

She takes her bra off, starts to dance and everyone stands silently looking at her.

I say, 'All I've come for is my key,' and put my plonker back in.

She dances some more, puts her clothes back on and then goes.

'Was that sixty quid's worth?' I ask the Italian.

'It's gooda-value,' he says. 'Gooda-value.'

'What? A fiver to have your plonker pulled out!'

'Donta-worry,' he says, tapping my face. 'Now if you give me twenty-five pounds. . . .'

I searched Martin, by this time insensible, plucked the room key from his pocket, made my excuses and left.

The Cyprus connection

At least on Foreign Trips like that you do finally get a bed for the night. Not so in the RAF.

When I went to entertain the troops in Cyprus the only transport was in the hold of a Hercules from RAF Lyneham in Wiltshire. It was about as comfortable as spending six hours in a dustbin with a punk rock band.

I arrived for the flight at 9 p.m., only to be told that take-off wouldn't be until three o'clock the next morning. At midnight I was issued with a pass to go to the 'Wessex Restaurant' for food. This place is like a café with a 'good' side and a 'bad' side, which look exactly the same. And the only thing they're serving is breakfast.

The duty man is a Cockney sergeant who has a group of Iranian pilots queueing on one side: 'Don't worry,' he says to me. 'I'll just see this little lot orf first.'

I stand there, not much bothered, because I've got a three-hour wait anyway. He shouts to the Iranians: 'All right, then, come and get it.'

The pilots are peering into the containers and not choosing anything.

'Come on,' shouts the sergeant, 'it'll be bloody morning before we know it.'

The Iranians are talking between themselves and pointing.

'Get your hands off that food,' roars the sergeant.

'Excuse me,' says one of the pilots. *'No pork.'*

'This is the breakfast menu, there ain't no bleeding pork!'

'We do not eat pork.'

'There's no bleeding pork here – just bacon and sausage and spam!'

'No, but we...'

'Whatsamatter with pork? You Jewish?'

'How about some salad, please?'

'Salad! Salad? You don't have bleeding salad for breakfast. Here, have the bleeding sausage – there's not much pork in that.'

He's waving pork sausage, oozing grease and fat, in front of their noses and they are petrified, up against a barrier. Finally this sergeant grabs a telephone and screams something inaudible into it. After about a minute's total silence an officer arrives: 'Any problems, sergeant?'

'Yes sir,' he says. 'I'm having trouble with the gollies!'

RAF bases

RAF bases are supposed to be a comic's dream. But whenever I've had trouble it's been on an RAF base.

I went to do a pre-Christmas show one year at RAF Leckenfield near Hull where everyone was in full regimental dress. All the wives are in long gowns, everything is very formal, they've been going since seven o'clock in the evening and they've scoffed a four-course meal. Then this gink from Birmingham comes on at one o'clock in the morning who's telling them stories about Spaghetti Junction. He's supposed to be a comic, but he doesn't tell jokes. It must have seemed like a lecture. The only laughs I got were from the two disc jockeys behind me who were roaring.

Sudden death in the greyhound stadium

But the smallest audience I've played to was organized by a bloke in Portsmouth called Jon Isherwood.

Jon was a nice guy but trouble seemed to find him. If there was a knock on the door he would rush up to me, put a finger to his lips and then you would both have to hide behind the sofa. He'd never give you a reason.

He always had problems: money, wives, people who were going to do something for him letting him down. When he was seventeen he decided to be a cowboy and went around performing in Portsmouth country and western clubs where he would always have a good drink at each. One night, on the third or fourth stop, he threatened to piss over the front row of the audience and was actually all ready to do it. For the next week his phone rang itself off the wall with people cancelling bookings.

John hired a greyhound stadium to put on a massive folk festival which was expected to attract in the region of 15,000. He signed big groups, distributed 100,000 leaflets along the south coast, took out pages in local newspapers and built a huge stage with a pailing fence to keep the crowd away.

It started at two o'clock in the afternoon.

At three o'clock there were forty-six paying customers.

I went on and there was a group of six families picnicking around the bottom of the pailing. The rest of the audience, plus the artists, were in the bar.

In the early days I would do anything and everything. Firstly, for money. Secondly, for experience.

Having done one show very well in a folk club I had a couple of guys approach me who said they were from Aviers Teas and Coffees. There was an annual convention of the catering association of Great Britain which was taking place at the Palace Hotel, Buxton. Would I go along and be their 'surprise artist'?

It was a really posh affair: bats round your throat and gownless evening straps. They wanted me to wear a suit, take a guitar and they would provide the sound equipment. I went on after the dance band had been playing for a solid two hours ... 'Aviers Teas and Coffees would like to announce a surprise guest for the evening – Jasper Carrott!' There was a ripple of apathy.

Everyone was sitting around the sides of the dance floor and there was a huge gap in front of me. The microphone was on a stand with the cord stretched to its fullest extent and the mike was forty-five degrees to the stand. After half a minute of trying to get my mouth level with the mike and after a very near case of decapitation, someone came on and took it from the stand.

By this time apathy had swelled to total disinterest.

Someone eventually tried to get people from the tables to stand in front of me to add a bit of atmosphere and hissed: 'Do Hava Nagila'!

'What about the mike?'

'I'll hold it,' he says.

So I start doing 'Hava Nagila' – which is a funny song – and all the audience, instead of sitting and listening, get up to dance. A complete, miserable flop which Aviers Teas and Coffees were terribly embarrassed about. And to crown it all? The real downer? Their rivals, A. K. Brown Caterers Limited then brought on *their* surprise act for the night ... Mike Yarwood! The place went bonkers and within two and a half seconds were in absolute fits of laughter.

It was as much as I could do to write all his jokes down.

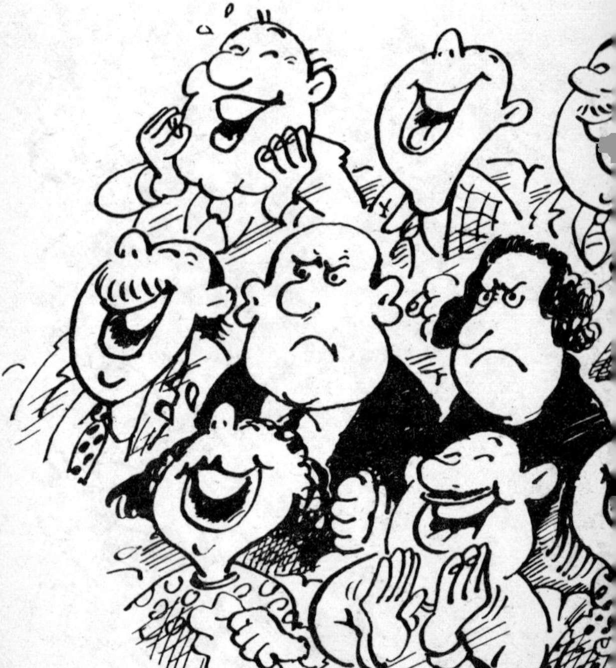

8 Personal Appearances and More Disasters

This ain't Shakespeare

Personal appearances can be like a drug. It gives you a whiff of fame, signing autographs and records, and seeing queues form around. That's why I agreed to go to Southampton.

Their biggest department store had been advertising that I was due to sign albums in their record department, so I drove into the back trade entrance to avoid the crowds.

The manager was there, wearing a polite but not over-enthusiastic expression on his face, with a handful of staff who are making formal conversation.

'What time's the presentation?' I ask.

The manager glances at his watch: 'About twelve-thirty.' It was already 12.35 p.m.

'Hadn't we better get out, then?'

'Relax. Don't worry about it yet.'

Another ten minutes goes by and I say: 'We really ought to start now, don't you think?'

The manager looks at me as if to say 'If you insist'.

We walk out and there are hundreds of Jasper Carrott albums – great piles of them – all over the place. And there was no one, no one at all, in the record department. People were coming through the door, wandering in, taking a look at the posters and pushing off again.

The management were ringed around me, looking and thinking: 'Who is this gink?'

I ended up signing a couple of records for the staff – who got them cut-price anyway – and the manager then took me out for a meal: 'Don't worry,' he says. 'Saturday is always a bad day....'

Not to be discouraged by this I went through the same agony at a record shop in Canterbury High Street.

I arrived late, marched straight into the shop, went to see the manager and hold out my hand: 'Jasper Carrott,' I say.

'Yeah,' he replies blankly, 'we've got his album here.' And he pulls one from a huge pile and hands it to me: 'Three pounds sixty-five,' he says.

I put the album next to my face and it slowly dawns on him who I am. I think we had five people asking me to sign the albums on that occasion.

In the end I was serving behind the counter and quaffing the free champagne they'd laid on.

But Coventry was the classic.

Woolworth's in Coventry on a Wednesday afternoon – the only shop open on half-day closing.

The local manager fancied himself as a disc-jockey and he had organized a crowd of women, with headscarves and shopping bags, surrounding a dais. They'd never heard of Jasper Carrott and were anticipating a Stork-tasting contest.

Then the manager announces: 'Ladies and gentlemen ... presenting – *Jasper Carrott!*' I then had to walk the length of the store to about twelve people and by this time he's saying: 'Come on. Come on, then. Well, give him a round of applause, at least.'

He then stands next to me cracking jokes for a full three minutes, with me looking around at twelve middle-aged women clutching their Co-op bags who couldn't have cared less whether I was walking naked along Coventry's shopping arcade.

You can never really tell how things are going to go.

I'd just returned from a trip to America and was due to play the Royal Shakespeare Memorial Theatre, Stratford-upon-Avon. I had seen a comedienne working in Los Angeles who had told a very funny sequence about this guy who was so keen to impress her that when making love he even went to the point of faking premature ejaculation. Then she said she knew he was going off her because when they went to bed he'd skip all the foreplay and go straight to lighting the cigarette.

I thought this little routine I could use at Stratford with an avant-garde audience, with me reversing the roles and telling the joke from the man's side.

I delivered the line about premature ejaculation and I have never heard a stonier silence. Seventy per cent didn't understand it, twenty per cent understood it but didn't think it very funny and ten per cent thought it was funny but were too scared to laugh. . . . I learned a lesson: Don't overestimate your audience. Most of all, don't overestimate yourself.

Wherever you work there's *always* someone in the audience who won't laugh. I have often pondered why and who these people are. They have paid to come in – usually in the best seats on the first two rows – but will *not* crack their faces. The women are probably wives of motor spares salesmen; the men I don't know.

And it's like a fly to a lightbulb. You can't help but keep on looking at them. Others can be falling around holding their sides, tears streaming down their face, mouths open wide, but their lips are set in a thin line like compressed concrete.

I remember one time this bloke sitting in a club two rows back. I thought he was made of wax. His face had not moved once, let alone to laugh. I'd also had one in the night before, so I was getting a bit pissed off with it all. So at the end of the first half of the show I thought I would go over and say something. I thought: I'll go up and ask what he's doing here. Why pay good money to come and see an act you obviously don't like? Why have a thoroughly miserable time like that?

I walked up to him and was just about to let rip when he turned around to this bird who was with him and said: *'Qu'est-ce qu'il dit? Je ne comprends pas un seul mot. . .'*

Warrington

Sometimes it can be the other way round. You can get a guy who is *too* keen. It was six o'clock on a Sunday night in Warrington.

Now Warrington is known for three things – the glass factory, their vodka and Eddie Waring saying 'War-er-rr-ing-*ton*' in his commentaries on rugby league.

John Starkey was with me and I was due on at the Civic Hall at eight o'clock. We got to the centre of town and the only living being seemed to be a woman standing at a bus stop. John put down the electric window of the car and asked her where the hall was.

He'd hardly got the words out when a drunk lurched from a shop doorway, stuck his head through the window and says: 'I think you're fantastic, Jasper ... you're one of us ... great, I've seen all your telly programmes ... heard all your records ... great ... can you give me a lift to the Civic Hall?'

We just about managed to get some directions from the woman, push this drunk's head out and get on our way: 'God, that was a close thing,' says John.

We took off round a complex one-way street system – you know the type, it takes you two miles to do 300 yards – and get to the Civic Hall about fifteen minutes later. As we pull up outside the stage door this drunk totters towards us again: 'Jasper! You're one of the best ... great ... I've seen your shows ... great ...

put it there, pal!' He was walking in after us and the hall's staff were asking: 'Is he with you?'

There was John, myself, two roadies and four staff from the hall and *no one* would do anything about this drunk. He was a big bugger and we were all scared. I ensconced myself in the dressing room, locked the door while this guy was banging on it: 'Hey, Jasper ... great ... just a minute, like ... there's something I want to say.'

I was standing there petrified and thinking: 'I hope he doesn't get in here.' Then there was silence. I put my ear to the door to listen – and suddenly he bursts in through the connecting door from another dressing room.

He had a ridiculous, insensible conversation like: 'The light's shining on my legs. I can't get rid of the light ... but I think you're great, Jasper ... fantastic ... Ace!'

I had some beer on a table, courtesy of the Civic Hall, so I pick up a bottle and use it to entice him out of the dressing room. He follows, sniffing, as if I'm holding up a fat steak and he hasn't eaten for a week.

I'd got visions of him leaping up on stage during the show, sitting waiting for us in our car, following us home, staying the night – everything. And all the time shouting: 'Jasper ... great!' and never becoming sober.

Coronation Street meets Crossroads

I wonder if 'Coronation Street' stars ever have such problems?

I've always wanted to do a television show: 'Coronation Street Coach Trip to the Crossroads Motel'. It would give me the chance to kill off all the characters in one go. The coach would crash into the motel just as a terrorist is planting a bomb and the only thing they'd find afterwards is Albert Tatlock's jock-strap.

My missus loves 'Coronation Street', much to my shame. And because it's on I get involved with it and start asking 'Here, what happened to Elsie Tanner's bloke?' I start picking up on it all and watching this programme when I'm surrounded by books on Shakespeare and Einstein. In 'Coronation Street' there might be an imminent death and you're expecting it on the Monday and they keep you waiting – so you have to watch the death on the Wednesday. And there's always complications so you have to watch the following Monday again to find out who got what.

I suppose the most compulsive example of addiction is that Tony Blackburn videotapes 'Crossroads'!

I'm a bit of a TV addict. That's why I was delighted to be told I had won a TV Award.

It was puzzling, though. Most local television stations didn't even show my series until after the epilogue. I remember ATV – the Birmingham station – putting it on at 11.30 p.m. *after* an hour-long programme on Jewish Chamber Music. So when I turned up at the London hotel for the award I heard people asking: 'Who the hell is he?'

At least Larry Adler knew. He gave me a tiny mouth organ. He said nurses love them. They just stick them in the patients' mouths when they go to sleep at night and so long as they're making a noise breathing into the harmonica they know they're still alive.

Then a week later, another award. The fallacy of it all is that you're not supposed to know you've won. You have to pretend to be surprised. I wanted to come on in a shower jacket with a shower cap and toothpaste foaming around my mouth and say: 'If I was to say to you that this has come as a complete surprise . . .' But they banned that because it would give the game away.

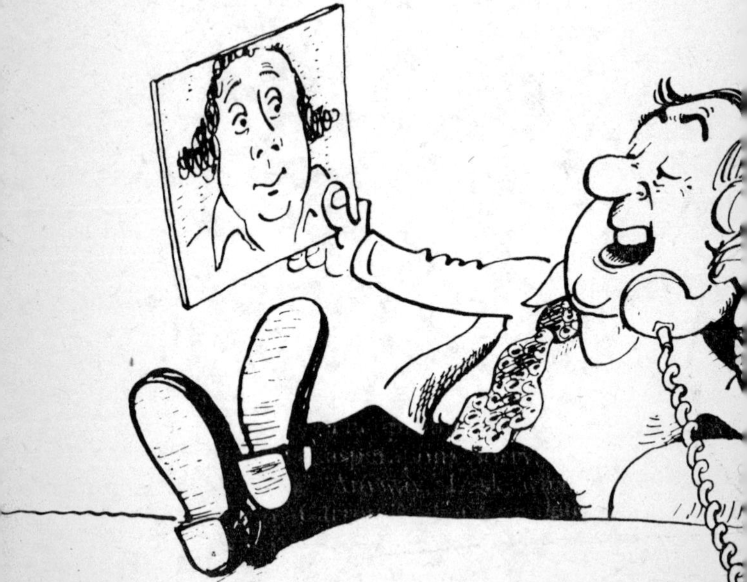

9 We Like It—But It Will Never Sell

'Magic Roundabout'

I'd never been near a TV studio when I made a private album called 'Jasper Carrott in the Club' which had a picture of me on the cover standing outside Mothercare with a pillow up my jumper.

I sent it to all the record companies and everyone said the same thing: 'We like it – but it will never sell.' But whenever I tried to get it back – because the albums were costing me a lot of money – it was always a case of: 'Oh, the secretary's borrowed it.' And when you traced the secretary she'd have lent it someone else. So for an album that had no chance of selling it was being listened to by a lot of people.

Now the strange thing about the music business is that they are always looking for something that's just happened. When Slade were successful they were looking for another Slade. Right now they're all looking for another Kate Bush.

So when Billy Connolly became successful with his live album DJM Records signed me up. They gave me £1000 and suggested I do a single. I had a song called 'Little Big Bike' which we decided to change to 'Funky Moped' and recorded it in Birmingham with Bev Bevan on drums and Richard Tandy, also of Electric Light Orchestra, on keyboards. Jeff Lynne, ELO's songwriter and singer, produced it. I'd spent £700 of DJM's thousand – so when they asked me what I was going to put on the 'B' side I was stumped. I'd completely forgotten about that!

So rather than go back in the studio I decided to put 'Magic Roundabout' on, which was already on my home-made album. Sure enough, 'Funky Moped', which I did in a Birmingham accent, was picked up, and the record got to the sixties in the charts. But the disc-jockeys were buying up 'Magic Roundabout' and it was a huge hit in the discos, where everyone would stop and listen.

It was one of the least-played records on the radio which has ever become a hit. It finally made the top five and sold 400,000.

The British Market Research Bureau refused to place the single at first because they were uncertain about what was going on. They put it at 50, then 45 and suddenly it came straight in at 13. All the disc-jockeys at the BBC wondered what the record was doing in the charts: someone had a copy and they played it. They were still no better off. Not one of them thought to turn over the record and play the 'B' side.

Here, for the benefit of those who didn't buy the record, is the script:

'Hello, children. It's a quarter to six. Time today for 'Magic Roundabout...!'
'I wonder where Florence is?' said Dougal.
'I'm over here,' said Florence.
'Hello, Florence,' said Dougal.
'Hello, Dougal,' said Florence.
Boing!
'Hello, Florence and Dougal,' said Zebadee.
'Hello, Zebadee.' said Dougal and Florence.
'Hello, Zebadee, Florence and Dougal,' said Dillon.
'Hello, Dillon,' said Zebadee, Florence and Dougal.
'I say,' said Dillon.
'What?' said Dougal.
Booinngg!
'Pardon?' said Zebadee.

'Nothing,' said Dougal.
'I wasn't talking to you,' said Zebadee.
'Oh,' said Dougal.
'Dillon,' said Dougal.
'Yes,' said Dillon.
'I wonder if Florence is a virgin?'
'Drops 'em for certain,' said Dillon.
Booinngg!
'That's right enough,' said Zebadee.
'How do you know?' said Dillon.
Booinngg!!
'To my knowledge half of Toytown knows of her horizontal pleasures. Let's face it, Noddy's the biggest ram round here and he reckons he's scored,' said Zebadee.
'I can hear you,' said Florence. 'It's not true. Noddy and I are just good friends.'
'Rubbish,' said Dougal. 'It's all over the canteen. Anyone knows about you, you brazen hussy.'
'You lousy old flea-bag,' said Florence 'Call yourself a dog? I've seen better hair on a lavatory brush!'
Booinngg!!
'Now look here,' said Zebadee, 'things are getting out of hand. Let's get back to the story-line!'
'It's a crummy story anyway,' said Dillon stubbornly.
Booinngg!
'No, it's not,' said Zebadee commandingly.
'Who cares?' said Dillon dejectedly.
'Well, I like it,' said Florence, hopefully.
'That's obvious!' said everybody, cockily.
Booinngg!
'Now look,' said Zebadee, 'let's try and get it together.'
'Well, I'm not working for that fat bat any more,' said Dougal. 'I'm off to join the Flowerpot men.'
'Good riddance,' said Florence.
'Knickers!' said Dougal.
'That's no way to talk to a lady,' said Dillon (knowing he's on to a good thing).
'Some lady!' said Dougal.
'Oh, piss off,' said Dillon.
And Dougal did so, all over Florence.
'Thank you for sticking up for me,' said Florence.
'Oh, it's nothing, really,' said Dillon.

'You know I've fancied you for a long time,' said Florence.
'I've fancied you, too,' said Dillon.
'Where do we go from here?' said Florence.
Booinngg!!!'

'Top of the Pops'

Now, we had all talked about 'Top of the Pops' and had *all* agreed – myself, my manager and DJM – that if it came up I definitely would *not* do it. I wasn't a 'Top of the Pops'-type artist, 'Funky Moped' wasn't selling the record and there should be no sell-out of our principles.

But when it got to number 13 Robin Nash of 'Top of the Pops' called the record-plugger at DJM – who had been having a very hard time as nothing from DJM had been selling except Elton John – and announced: 'I want Jasper Carrott on "Top of the Pops".'

The plugger said: 'There's no way he'll do it.'

Nash replied: 'But I want him.'

The plugger thought, my job's on the line here. If I don't get Jasper Carrott how am I ever going to get anyone else on that programme because I've upset Robin Nash?

So the plugger comes to me: 'Will you do "Top of the Pops"?'

'Forget it,' I tell him. 'I'm a comic.'

He pleads: 'You've got to do it.'

'No. I don't want to.'

'You'll get 50,000 extra sales from an appearance, it will go straight into the top five and you'll be worth a fortune.'

CHING!

'Maybe,' said I, 'I will do "Top of the Pops".'

My only condition was that he get me a white suit, white shoes and a blue shirt.

'Anything!' gasps the plugger.

They would at that point have given me Prince Charles's ears.

I also laid down one extra condition: that there would not, definitely not, be a moped in the studio. And there was no way that I would ever sing this song sitting on a moped.

'Sure, Jasper,' he says. 'Anything. Absolutely anything.'

I had seen Mike Harding on the programme a week before – a coincidence because we're both from the folk club circuit – singing 'Rochdale Cowboy'. They'd got him dressed up as a cowboy sitting on an alsatian dog.

Just before I set off I called the record plugger again: 'Definitely no moped is there?'

'No, no, no, no. Definitely *not*.'

The first thing I see when I get to the BBC studio? A gleaming great moped right in the middle of the stage. And the first question they asked? 'Where's your moped gear?'

So I am then treated to a one-way conversation from a guy with a hand two-way radio: 'Jasper Carrott says he's not sitting on the moped. . . . Well, that's what he says. . . . Well, he hasn't brought his moped gear. . . . Well, fuck you!'

Rehearsals for the various acts drag on all afternoon. When I come on there are exactly six minutes left before the end of rehearsal time. I finish my first take and there was a deathly silence in the studio. You could see every technician, every cameraman, every sound man, the floor manager, the producer, the band, the back-up vocalists – everyone – all thinking: 'What the fuck is this? This is never going out in a million years.'

There are just two people running around the studio yelling 'Great! Fantastic' – Robin Nash and my record plugger.

I can see the whole of my career, built up over years of graft, being destroyed in three minutes;

'Let's give it another try,' shouts the floor manager, and off we go again.

This time, it's even worse. Then, six o'clock comes. End of rehearsal time. *Finish*. The union men are off, so we're now into the proper show.

I stalk off to the bar and Robin Nash follows: 'Try it just once,' he says. 'If it's no good I promise we'll not put it out on the air.'

So, with my white suit, I do this real send-up of myself. Sex-image projection. Style. Panache. Staring deep into the camera. The kids hadn't got the faintest idea what was going on and just look at me dumbly.

They had to turn on taped applause. . . . .

DJM Records decided to make a film for 'Top of the Pops' on me so there would be no repeat of this farce. They would illustrate scenes from 'Funky Moped'.

Typical of the record industry, I had a call from a finger-snapping promotion guy called Colin Stone at six o'clock one night and he says: 'Be in London tomorrow morning to make a film.'

I turn up and nothing has been organized. We have to go out in the street to look for greasers on motorbikes. I stop alongside one guy and ask him if he wants to be in a film.

'Yeah, okay,' he says with about as much enthusiasm as if I'd asked him to give me a tow. We get another motorcyclist in the same way and then commandeer a milk float.

Colin Stone stops traffic in the middle of a main road during rush-hour and when people ask what it's all about simply says: 'Top of the Pops!' as if that explained everything. The remarkable thing was, everyone accepted it as an explanation for being jammed in their cars for about an hour.

We also took over a café and pub in the course of the afternoon. Everyone was as helpful as if we'd asked them to contribute their time to save the lives of six men.

The light is fading, but we've finished the film apart from fitting in the line at the end of 'Funky Moped' when I sing: 'Me mum won't let me mend it in the kitchen, I've got to fix it in the garden.' We need someone to pose as my mum, and throw out all this motorbike gear after me.

'Don't worry,' says Colin Stone, 'we'll get my mother to play the part.' His mum's house is very handy in Islington, so we all race round there.

'Oh no,' she says. 'I couldn't do anything like that. I don't want to be on any film.'

Colin starts moaning at her. We had, after all, been dragging people from the streets all afternoon and they hadn't objected. So she says: 'Hold on. I know a neighbour who's a great sport. She'll be Jasper's mum.'

We all breathe a sigh of relief because there's only a few minutes of light left. Then Colin's mum returns with the neighbour. She's as black as the ace of spades.

The film remained unfinished and unused.

Colin Slade, walking dynamo

Colin Stone was one of those guys who'd try anything. A walking dynamo.

DJM had a record out called 'The Womble-Bashers of Wimbledon' by Grimms. Grimms included John Gorman of 'Scaffold'. So Colin decides to organize a promotion gimmick of getting dressed up as a Womble, having John as a Womble-basher and then invading the centre court while they're televizing Wimbledon tennis. The Womble-basher would race around the centre court, bashing Colin around the head.

It involved buying two black market tickets for the centre court at a cost of about £200. They both turn up with bundles of clothes ready to get dressed up for this gimmick. But when they get inside they find themselves staring down at the court from about half a mile away. Their seats are about three rows from the back.

John says: 'This is a non-starter.'

'No, you're all right,' Colin assures him. 'Stay cool.'

So they both sneak off to the toilet to get changed as a Womble and a Womble-basher before returning to their seats to await their chance. As soon as there's a break in the tennis, Colin leaps up and says: 'Come on, let's get on the court.'

They both get as far as the first security guard who simply sticks an arm across the two of them, doesn't even raise an eyebrow at the way they're dressed, and says: 'You can't go any further.' They were still about fifty yards from the court so they couldn't even make a dash for it.

It ends up with John chasing Colin up and down rows of seats with people in the crowd ignoring them completely. There are no cameras around, no reporters, no publicity. Nothing. They carry on until they both feel exhausted because it's so hot in their costumes and just slink back to the seats.

Everyone in the crowd just carry on eating their strawberries and cream.

Jester Carrott

But then record companies will do anything for a new angle.

I was invited to London to do a promotion called 'The Two Sides s asper Carrott'. The idea was that I should wear a business suit and a jester's suit and with a bit of trick photography they could split it down the middle and present one picture with half of me in business clothes and the other half in a jester's.

I arrive there early one morning to be met by a promo guy who says: 'Hi, man. Right. This is gonna be great. Let's go.'

We spent two hours trying to find the photographers.

Eventually, we get there down a cul-de-sac, from a mews, from a square which is off a crescent. In the photographer's studio is a jester's outfit which must have seen every Dick Whittington pantomime since 1936. There's a grease smear down one leg, buttons are missing and there is only one bell out of three on the hat.

'Right,' he says. 'Now where's your business suit?'

'I don't own a business suit.'

The promo guy hits his head with his hand in exasperation: 'Sorry! I forgot to mention that.'

'Anyway,' I ask, what is this "Two Sides of Jasper Carrott"?'

'Your comic side and your serious side,' he replies.

'What serious side?'

'Your songs.'
'But I don't do any serious songs.'
'Oh you don't? Well . . . no problem.'

It ends up with me, wearing a pair of jeans and denim jacket and borrowing the photographer's tie to have the 'serious' picture taken. Then I get dressed in the tatty jester's outfit for the 'comic' side.

No one has *ever* figured out what the 'Two Sides of Jasper Carrott' really were – but a campaign was launched. Posters. Advertisements. The lot!

The pop business is like throwing mud on a wall and hoping some of it sticks.

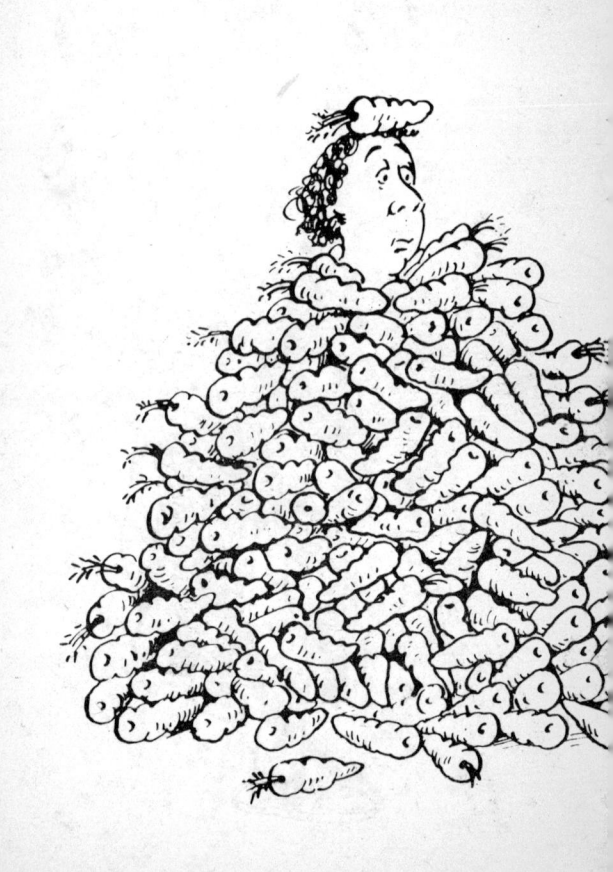

10 The Other Side of the Camera

Smile, please!

What I can't stand about photographers is that they all think that they are being terribly individual. Yet basically there are two types. One is in a tweed jacket and has a pipe clenched between his teeth. The other has a Christian Dior set of overalls with the name of a rock band emblazoned on the back. One is functional, the other arty. But they both produce exactly the same type of photograph.

'You're a comedian,' they say. 'Pull a funny face.'

A comic can not possibly be seen as being serious.

Newspapers send photographers to our home from London, two and a half hours each way. They then spend two hours reorganizing your household, moving furniture while all the time you're trying to hide your children or anything personal in case they get hold of it. They have you riding kid's bikes, climbing up trees, putting your head up the fireplace.

And the end result? An inch-square picture of your head.

I always look like a mental moron on photographs. I never used to worry, but I've seen things that've changed my mind. People have asked: 'Is that you?' Or: 'Were you ill?' Or: 'Are you better now?'

Of course, a photographer looks at the world through a very narrow view: the lens. They sit on their backsides at soccer matches in the rain, get spat upon or trampled by the goalie and risk getting hit by flying bottles. What sort of life is that? I think it weakens the brain for when they come to see me.

One of them had me pretending to eat a plate!

They've had me standing on top of the roof, going up in a helicopter, driving a vintage car, flying in a balloon. And in the studio, whatever you do or however you pose, it's always . . . 'That's fantastic – great, fine – do that again – do that some more – brilliant, marvellous, wonderful . . .' And the pictures are *still* the same.

But every photographer always starts by getting out a carrot with his camera. The carrot is usually either very large or has an unusual shape. I've had carrots up my nose, in my ears, I've had them chewed, grated, cubed, mashed.

Then there's the variations for a 'new' angle: swedes, cabbages, leeks. They turn up with sackfuls of carrots, wagon-loads of carrots, even vanfuls of carrots.

Any day now I'm expecting some photographer to arrive driving an articulated truck packed with thirty tons of carrots which he wants to cascade down on me and take a picture while I'm smiling.

Scarface

Of course, I have to admit it, another reason I don't like photographs is that they always show up my scar.

If you have a scar on your face there are two reactions. People I've known for years might never even mention it, or when they do they wonder at er, ummm, how I, if you don't mind, acquired such an unfortunate disfigurement.

Others are introduced for the first time: 'How do you do? How the hell did you get that bloody scar?' Or: 'Made a right mess of your face, that. Can't you get something done about it?'

The first time I met Eric Morecambe he just looked at it and said: 'Heidelberg?'

It depends.

Sometimes I got it saving a young girl from eight rapists and twelve muggers in Cannon Hill Park.

Other times I had a fight with the leader of the Slash End Kids razor gang.

Occasionally it was in a duel; once or twice it's been simply another mouth growing.

But whatever the explanation there is always one inevitable outcome: people show me *their* scars. And it doesn't matter where we are. Be it in restaurants, on buses or in the street they have no hesitation in stripping off and letting me examine in minute detail bullet wounds from the Somme or where they were bitten by a wild stoat.

Sometimes you can get whole groups of people performing Yoga-like positions while arguing as to who has the most horrifying deformity. I've seen some pretty ugly sights including Malcolm MacDonald's legs which look as if they've been used as kicking posts by football hooligans; a commissionaire who had been attacked by a Sex Pistols fan; and a Glaswegian with a four-foot gash on his abdomen, acquired, he said, during a post-mortem.

But it's not just scars. They can be birthmarks, zits, moles, warts – and all shown eagerly and without a trace of embarrassment. Somehow a scar has no sexual overtones at all, wherever it is. They think because I've got a scar I'm some sort of expert.

And how did I really get mine?

Would you believe a bloody great dog attacked me when I was six?

I was defending the house from a vicious gang of sabre-rattling pirates at the time!

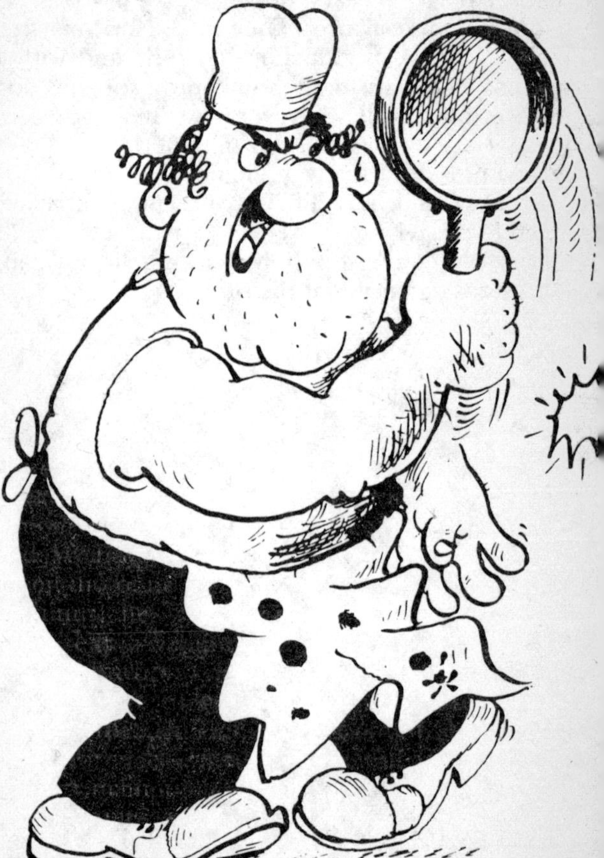

11 From Motorways to Moles

Motorway chefs

They start in the RAF, then they're sent to the army and finally to a holiday camp.

But the real accolade of being the worst all-time chef is to graduate to a motorway service station.

Only then, with arms pasted up to the elbow with grease, can they get beefburgers like ice hockey pucks. They can even destroy Heinz baked beans. You can break your jaw on their soft-boiled eggs.

I always imagine that a top motorway chef rejects beefburgers and sausages on the grounds that they are too soft and can, with effort, be bitten.

And the people that clean up! They use rags you wouldn't use on your car engine. When they have cleaned the tables you can guarantee they are protected for a month with a quarter-inch layer of unmovable fat.

You know why they get drunks at motorway service cafés when they don't even serve alcohol? It's the only way customers can summon enough courage to face the food.

You get those sandwiches like cotton wool wads with Sunlight soap in the middle. I've quite often washed my hands at a motorway service station with a lump of cheese! They put the cheese in the toilets and the soap in the sandwiches and defy people to tell the difference.

But there's always something to challenge your ingenuity. Tomato sauce bottles in the shape of tomatoes which are so bunged up with gunge you have to chip your way through to get to the entrance. But the real test is to get to the sauce successfully without spilling it over the table in one great dollop.

The only reason I stop at motorway cafés these days is to remind me to keep on driving. It's also an incentive to take my wife's sandwiches.

The wine expert

The manager who runs my favourite restaurant had a salesman in last year offering him an exclusive on Beaujolais Nouveau. He could have it on 14 November – before France, according to this salesman.

So the manager orders sixteen cases of the stuff and places a huge advert in the local papers which screamed: 'SCOOP – November 14th Beaujolais Nouveau arrivé.'

It was a packed restaurant that night but no one, absolutely no one, ordered Beaujolais Nouveau. Just before closing a party of six arrived and asked to see the wine list. The manager, desperate, said: 'You can see the wine list, sir. But this morning we have our first shipment – totally exclusive and at great expense – of Beaujolais Nouveau.'

'Oh, really?' said this guy. 'What year?'

Of course, we have to eat out a lot in our house.

Hazel asks: 'Do you want a sandwich?' and three hours later you'll get it. She'll ask if you want fish and then you suddenly see her driving down the road and don't see her again for half a day.

The worst thing we did was get the freezer. She always gets bread that's as cold as ice and makes sandwiches. It's a shock when we get fresh bread from a baker.

'Mummy,' protest the kids. 'This bread is all soft and warm!'

The Girt Clog Climbing Club

Whenever I'm away on tour I always try and get back to my wife Hazel and three children, Lucy, Jenny and Hannah, even if it means driving for hours through the early morning after a late concert.

I can always sleep in and motor to the next gig during the afternoon. I just prefer not to waste long days sitting around hotel rooms or propping up the bar alone.

There is, however, one exception. The Girt Clog Climbing Club Annual General Meeting.

This is the one time of the year I leave my wife and kids and sample the clean, fresh, healthy sport of climbing in the Lake District. At least, that's how it started ten years ago. A group of keen young men from the industrial Midlands seeking the open-air life, camping, walking and enjoying the scenery.

But over the years, with the coming of marriages and mortgages, this weekend has deteriorated into a couple of nights away from The Wife during which you can get as much ale down your gullet as possible.

It has grown from just a small group of friends into a massive Masonic-like society of thirty or thirty-five which meets from all over the country to revert to childhood in a place called the Saury Hotel. In the early days we used to walk at least eight hours every Saturday and drink for a couple of hours during the evening. Now the process is exactly the opposite.

We also give each other delightful awards, like the Piss Head of the Year (heaviest drinker), The Bike of the Year (someone we know who's the easiest lay), and The Thrutch Award (series of sexual exploits).

During one particularly under-sexed year I won The Thrutch Award, simply for being the father of three children within four and a half years.

Sex supermarket

It was the closest I'd been to any sex award since they opened a sex supermarket in Solihull.

Ever been to Solihull? It makes Chelsea look common. It's ruled by an elite. Everybody talks as if they've got a tennis ball stuck in the corner of their mouths. All Tories, obviously. There was a Labour bloke once. But they hung him. The town is ruled by a collection of old biddies and one man, reputed to be 108.

So the guy who opened this sex supermarket must have been a genius. I was wandering round there for about a week. I couldn't believe some of the stuff they had in there.

I bought a clockwork cucumber...'Made in Wigan' it said on the bottom.

All these old women were walking around outside with placards trying to get this place closed. 'Ban Sex', said the posters. 'Bring Back The Cat.' They saw me brandishing this clockwork cucumber: 'You dirty beast! You filthy swine! You give that here immediately! Hold this placard, Agnes. Agnes! *Agnes!* You must sign our petition. What's your name?'

'Carrott.'

'You filthy beast!'

Mole-in-the-hole

Anyway, I returned from the Girt Clog Club to find tha I'd got a mole making one hell of a mess of my garden.

I'd never come across them before. Born in Acocks Green you don't get a lot of moles around. If they found a mole in Acocks Green they'd eat it.

It took me just a few days to realize this mole was driving me bonkers. I'd spend hours and hours mowing the lawn and getting the lines all straight. Then next morning you wake up and it's like looking at a sea of zits. There just doesn't seem to be any mole-catchers left. So it's a DIY job with moles (Destroy It Yourself).

So I bought a mole trap: a big metal thing you have to bait with worms. A pretty revolting job, so I used spaghetti and hoped they wouldn't know the difference. But I put plenty of bait in the trap, set it and the mole came along, ate all the spaghetti and pushed the trap out of the way. It took me two months before I realized that there was no way he was going to go into it. He was just getting bigger on all the spaghetti he was eating.

Then I bought a firework, called Molesmoke, which is like a Roman candle. You light it, shove it down the hole and then cover the earth over. The instructions say: 'The smoke, which is heavier than air, lies in the run, is poisonous and kills the mole!'

No, it doesn't.

They love them. You can hear them giggling.

And after a while you begin to get the mole twitch.

'You got a mole?'

'Yeah,' you say, with a tick in your face.

People come up with loopy ideas of how to get rid of them. 'There's only one way to get rid of a mole – you've got to shove garlic and mothballs down the holes. They don't like the smell.'

'Really?'

'Never fails.'

So I was there for two weeks shovelling the stuff down. They ate the lot! Just got enormous moles and bigger hills.

Then this other bloke says: 'There's only *one* way to get rid of a mole.'

'What?'

'You've got to buy those plastic windmills you get from Woolworths.

'They are like long sticks with a plastic bit at the end which whirls around. You get one of them,' he says, 'and you stick it down the middle of the mole run. When the wind sends the whirly bit round it vibrates the stick and the noise scares the mole away.'

I fell for it.

I've got two hundred of them in my lawn.

The first big gust of wind blew my fence down, yet the moles, far from being frightened, ate all the ends of the sticks.

About five weeks ago I was in the local boozer having a drink when this guy comes in: "Ere,' he says. 'I 'ear you got a mole.'

'Yes.'

'There's only *one* way to get rid of a mole.'

'Really...'

'Blow its bloody head off!'

'What with?'

'A twelve-bore.'

'What do you do? Stick it down the hole and...'

'No, no,' he says, shaking his head. 'But it costs you a night's sleep, mind.'

'Anything. I'll sacrifice anything.'

'What you do is stay up all night. When it's all quiet Moley starts digging, pushing up the earth from your lawn. When he does that he's only half an inch from the top. Then you start blasting away.'

'Does it work?'

'Never fails!'

'But where do I get a twelve-bore from?'

'You can borrow mine for a fiver.'

Sure enough, he delivers the gun and a box of cartridges – enough to do a bank raid. I'm there on a Sunday night with this great big gun. I have strapped a torch to the barrel so I can see what I am doing. And I sit on a swivel chair.

All the neighbours are watching from their bedroom windows: 'What's he doing?'

'I don't know. Imitating a lighthouse?'

So it's about half past three on a Sunday morning and so quiet you could hear a leaf drop.

Suddenly I hear a scratching and five yards ahead there's a mole coming out of the lawn. I turn on the searchlight. Now, I know this sounds stupid, but I'd never thought to practice with the twelve-bore. I had never fired a gun that size in my life.

So... BOOM!

And I flew ten yards off my stool.

The only thing I hit were all the apples in my tree.

I was incensed and started shooting everywhere... BOOM! BOOM! BOOM!! Shooting like a maniac. The garden was like the Somme.

Then I noticed this blue flashing light. There were a couple of coppers standing there: 'What are you doing Carrott?'

'Mole-catching.'

They wander over. Luckily, one of them had suffered the ravages of a mole so was sympathetic. He muttered: 'Carry on. But be quiet.'

They're still there, of course, digging up the garden.

'What's on tonight?' 'Beetroot.' 'Oh, not so good as mothballs and garlic.' 'No. And we could do with some more fireworks to see what we're doing.' 'I wonder if we'll get any more wind-sticks again.' 'Hope so. They're delicious.' 'Bloody noisy up there last night, wasn't it?'

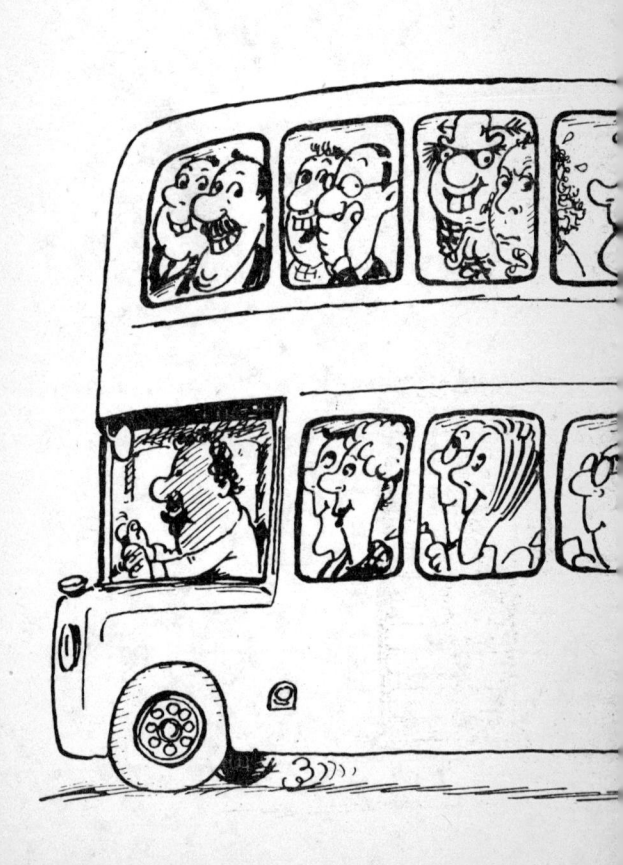

12 On the Buses

Dial-a-Bus

We live now next to what is known as a 'nice' area. In fact, it's so 'nice' it's got one of the biggest concentration of millionaires in the country outside Knightsbridge.

The average house price is around £60,000 and there are at least two cars in every garage. Each seventeen-year-old son has his own sports car. And if the kids are younger then they have chauffeurs to take them to private schools.

That is why it seemed that the world had gone mad when *this* area was selected for 'Dial-a-Bus'.

This was a special bus halfway between the size of a Thames truck and a transit. The bus would come to pick you up at the end of your road, or even at your house. All you had to do was telephone the head office and your message would be relayed to the bus driver's radio cab.

This was all to be subsidized by the taxpayer. But you know how this area was allocated what was a revolutionary system of public transport? Simply on the strength that there were more telephones per household than any other area in the country.

So the only people who end up using these buses are the cleaners and chauffeurs going between the big houses! It took officialdom a whole two years before they realized what was happening.

It would have been useful for the old people of the area. But the public telephone boxes were so scarce that by the time they had rung for the Dial-a-Bus and got back home, it had been and gone.

Insurance forms

It was a shame, because I've always felt a certain affiliation towards buses.

It was on a bus that I found a set of motor claim forms which were received by a large insurance company in London. When you have an accident this is the form you are sent with questions like: 'What speed were you doing at the time of the accident?'

Stupid question because everyone answers: 'Twenty-eight miles an hour.'

On the back is a big empty space which says: 'Give, in your own words, a description of how the accident occurred.'

This is where you get *your* chance to give *your* version of the accident – which, of course, is totally different to everyone else's.

This is what people wrote on those claim forms:

'The accident was due to an invisible lorry narrowly missing me.'

'I bumped into a stationary tree coming in the other direction.'

'I was scraping my near-side on the bank when the accident happened.'

'The other man altered his mind and I had to run over him.'

'I bumped into a lamp-post which was obscured by human beings.'

'Coming home I drove into the wrong house and collided with a tree I haven't got.'

'The accident was caused by me waving to the man I hit last week.'

'I blew my horn but it would not work as it was stolen.'

'I thought the side window was down, but it was up, as I found out when I put my bloody head through it.'

But the best one, I think, was: 'I knocked over a man, he admitted it was his fault and said that he had been knocked down before.'

Whisky bottle

It's easy to leave things on buses.

I remember when I was employed by the BBC in Birmingham to do a folk club show. The guy who was hiring me said: 'Right. You're going to have to have a medical now.'

The only medical I'd ever had was at school. And you know what school medicals are. They get through about 800 kids in half an hour. You just run through the gym with your tongue hanging out. If you fall over you're blind. You could have dysentery and beriberi but it would never show up in a school medical.

So I went to this medical and was going through all the normal things: gargling, chopping knees, coughing. And reading all those silly card things. All I could read was 'Printed by E J Robinson'. Right at the end the doctor said: 'Right, Mr Carrott. We're now going to do a urine test. You give me a sample of your urine.'

'But where?'

'In the beaker by the shelf. There,' he points.

It was a good twelve foot away. If he'd have given me a stool I might have stood a chance.

It was a bit unfortunate, really, because it was straight after lunch and I'd been celebrating something with a few of the lads. We'd got through about eight pints of Double Diamond each. Well, he should have had a bigger beaker.... When you start you can't stop, 'What the bloody hell are you doing?' he says.

It was brimming and frothing and he wouldn't pick it up. I wasn't going to help. I knew what was in it.

The litmus paper came out bright orange instead of blue.

'You may have diabetes,' he says gravely. 'You'll have to go for another check at the Queen Elizabeth Hospital tomorrow.'

'What?'

'Well,' he shrugs, 'it's just to make sure.'

'But what if I have got it?'

'Well,' he says, laying a reassuring hand on my shoulder, 'I should have a last fling tonight just in case.'

So I went mad. Double Diamonds, whisky, wine... curry. Pouring it down. Cramming doughnuts into my mouth. The next morning I felt so bad my teeth itched.

I was trying to find a bottle or jar to hold my urine so I could take it to the hospital. I'd got nothing, apart from an empty Johnny Walker scotch bottle, half size.

Fair enough. I filled it, put it in a bag, got on a bus, got off near the Queen Elizabeth Hospital, handed my card to the guy on the gate – and realized I'd left the bottle in the bag on the bus.

I thought: 'Oooh. Some poor bugger's in for that.' I've never got it back and I went round to every lost property office in Birmingham. I reckon someone grabbed hold of it and thought they'd have a little party.

'Cheers, Harry.'

Aaargh!

'Yes, wonderful blend, Harry!' Then, to his wife: 'Tastes just like piss, doesn't it?'

The Nutter

When you're on a bus and the Nutter gets on the bus, does the Nutter ever sit next to you?

The Nutter *always* sits next to me.

They're always on the number eleven route, too, aren't they?

You're sitting there, minding your own business, and the bus stops, a couple of people get on and it starts off again. Then you hear the Nutter coming up the stairs: ' 'ello, has anyone seen my camel?'

There's a strangled cry from everyone who scream to themselves: 'It's the Nutter! Please, God, don't let the Nutter sit next to me!'

Everyone starts stretching out on their seats.

If I'm on the bus I always get the Nutter next to me. I must have this sign above my head which says 'Nutter Lover'. They always sort me out in no time: 'This anyone's seat?'

'No. . . .'

'Oh, *good!*'

And you can hear the sighs of relief from everyone else on the bus: 'Thank God he's got the Nutter . . . it's a camel job as well . . . they're the worst. . . .'

And the Nutter starts showing you things: 'I've got an Atom Bomb here,' and he hands you a tin of corn beef.

Of course, once you've actually got the Nutter everyone else on the bus stretches back in their seats to enjoy it.

'Have you paid your fare?'

'Er, yes.'

'Those your tickets?'

'Yes.'

Then he grabs hold of them, rips them up, throws them in the air and starts gurgling how he just loves weddings.

And the trouble is, some Nutters never let you *off* the bus. . . .

I have spent up to three weeks on a bus with a nutter.

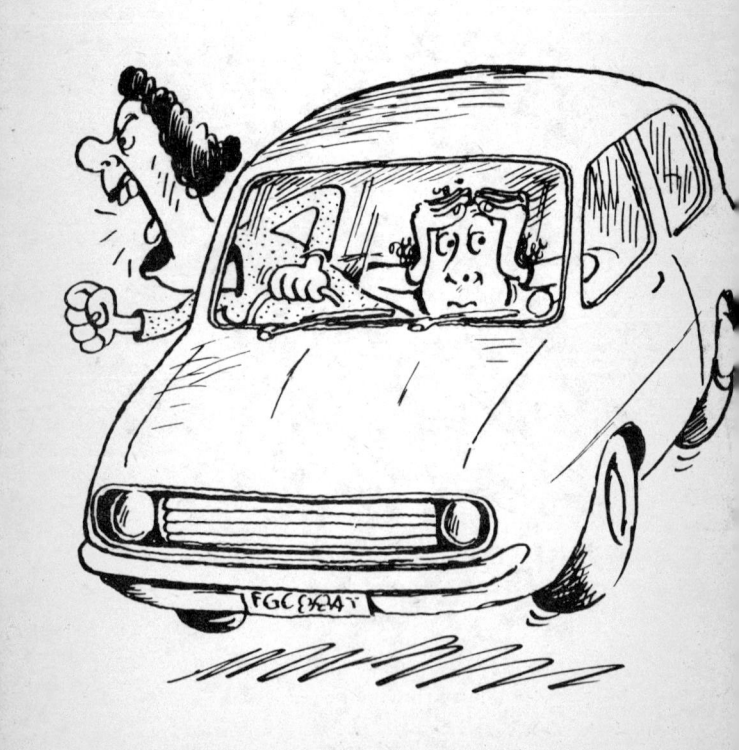

13 Driven to Distraction

Driver-in-law

Even worse is a nutter in the driver's seat. Especially in the form of my mother-in-law. Now I've nothing against women drivers – they're just like any other normal psychopath!

My mother-in-law drives but she hasn't passed her test. She's been driving since before the war and has gone through twenty-three tests which is an all-time record for Warwickshire. People told me about her driving but I never believed it. I thought it was being exaggerated. They say that you only take her out once as the qualified driver. She knows the Highway Code back to front, but she has a mind that cannot relate to why she's got to learn things.

The Highway Code states: 'You look into your rear-view mirror and then you pull out.'

So far as she's concerned it doesn't matter what's actually coming. Once she's looked into that rear-view mirror and obeyed the instructions, then it's safe to pull out.

She *never* changes down gear. The gear-stick to her is something for pumping oil into the servo-brake system.

We were going up a hill, in top gear, doing something like eleven miles an hour. The car was juddering so hard I thought it would never last.

With two inches to spare we made it to the top.

Then, she slams the car into second gear and roars

down, passing everything that's passed *us* on the way up.

She's been driving for forty years but has never had an accident.

She's *seen* hundreds.

Whenever I'm with her in the passenger seat – which is very rare – I try and jolly her along: 'You're a very good driver,' I tell her and this seems to stop her aiming the car like a bullet at other traffic.

But it didn't work recently. As I was congratulating her for the umpteenth time on keeping a straight course down a main road I vaguely noticed that some car had pulled up about half a mile ahead.

Suddenly, she slams her foot on the brake and I'm almost through the front window.

'What's the matter? What's happening?'

'It's *him*,' she says, pointing to the distant car. 'He didn't signal.'

Then she potters along, winds her window down and demands: 'What the bloody hell do you think you're doing?'

The guy, who by this time is about to enter his front door, is summoned by my mother-in-law. He walks over inquisitively.

'Road hog. Menace. Signal when you stop . . . it's in the Highway Code . . . people like you should take their test again . . . how dare you use the same road as me . . . you'll cause an accident before long. . . .'

Then, as I crawl from under the front seat to make sure the bloke isn't taking offence, she slams the car into third gear and then we go kangerooing on our chaotic way.

Parking ticket

If it had been me driving like that I know I would have been stopped within a hundred yards.

Why? Because I have *never* been able to break the law.

All the kids at school who went through a shoplifting phase used to take great lists of things they wanted, then go out and successfully nick them. Great tins of Victory-V lozenges ... battery torches ... diaries. I remember this one kid once who came back with a gross of diaries and was handing them around the class.

I got caught up in all this so I sidled up to Boots, nicked a fourpenny pencil sharpener and immediately felt a hand on my shoulder from a burly shop assistant: 'Oi,' he barks, 'Put that back!' He gives me a sharp clip around the ear and I just walk out of the shop again, empty handed.

It made me realize I would never be able to get away with a thing. I instantly feel guilty just thinking about it.

When I had my Lambretta scooter I also bought my first car, a Morris 1000. Not having enough money to tax the car I took the tax disc from the scooter and transferred it.

One night I went around to a friend's to collect a pile of records, stayed for some time and couldn't get the car started when I came out. It was a freezing cold night and the battery just died on me. So I left the car with a special side-light in the street parked near my friend's house. The local police station was fifty yards around a corner.

I got back the next morning and the car was *festooned* with tickets from the police, all flapping in the wind in their cellophane packets There were half a dozen on the windscreen, a couple on the roof, one on top of the aerial, another stuck in the front bumper.

And each one of these tickets carried a demand for me to go immediately to the police station.

I could just imagine all morning the station sergeant had been saying: 'Hello, George. Got an easy start for you here. There's an old Morris 1000 banger parked round the corner – go and find something wrong with it.'

I went in, saw the sergeant who had a face like thunder, and he holds up my tax disc: 'Where did you get this from, then?'

I was up before the magistrates in what seemed like ten seconds flat. . . . 'No tax and fraudulent use of a tax disc' was the charge.

I was absolutely petrified.

The case before mine was a couple of football hooligans and the police inspector was reading out, in a very serious voice, what one of them had said: 'The defendant walked up to me, your honour, and said: "Get off your fucking horse, Tonto, else I'll stuff this rattle straight up his arse." '

Yet these kids were really cool about it and slouched into the court – while I was shaking in my shoes.

They fined me fifteen quid and asked me how I'd like to pay.

'I haven't got a job at the moment,' I told them. 'Can I pay five shillings a week?'

'You're out of a job and yet you own both a car and a scooter,' snorts the magistrate. 'You'll pay in seven days.'

Jersey

I didn't have another brush with the law until I went to Jersey.

It was a few years ago and I had a call asking how were my bookings.

'I'm fully booked until tomorrow,' I told him.

Would I like to play in Jersey?

'Love it,' I said. 'How do I get there?'

'We'll fly you out.'

'And back in?'

'That,' he says, 'depends.'

I had never been to Jersey, so I thought I would fly out on the Sunday, do the booking on the Monday and return on Tuesday.

I get a couple of guys to meet me from the plane and start showing me around. By midnight I am as drunk as the newt. If you drink there comes a time in the stage of drinking when you know what you're going to do but you can't stop yourself.

I wandered into the middle of the main road and started directing traffic.

Within *seconds* there was a police car: 'What the bloody hell do you think you're doing?'

'Pardon?'

'What the bloody hell do you think you're doing?'

'I'm directing traffic.'

'The bloody traffic warden's supposed to do that.'

'Yes. But they're in bed, aren't they?'

I walked into a fish and chip shop and told these two guys who were with me what had happened: 'Don't upset the police in Jersey,' said one of them. 'Blimey! They'll crucify you.'

So I go out and start handing drivers fish and chips.

Fatal. The police are there again before I have a chance to swallow my first chip.

'Oi, you. Get in this car.'

'You're not having any fish and chips.'

'Get in the car!'

They took me to the charge room of the local station where there's a sergeant who has been in the force thirty years and has dealt with every drunk, itinerant, layabout and yobbo who has strayed into St Hellier. *Nothing* moves this guy.

'What have we got here?' he demands.

'He's been directing traffic in the middle of town,' says one of the policemen, 'and he's been giving drivers fish and chips.'

'Oh, has he? How long you lived here?'

'About five hours,' I reply.

'Comedian, eh!'

'Yes. How did you know?'

'What's your name?'

'Jasper Carrott.'

'Okay. You're gonna cause trouble. Cell number five.'

The owner of the folk club I was to play at came and bailed me out the next day. I also made the front pages of the local paper. In fact, it had its advantages. The club was packed out on the evening. They'd all come to see this maniac who had been directing traffic over the cliffs of St Hellier.

And laugh? They were terrified not to.

The boys in blue

These days I always get on with policemen and they call regularly at our house.

We used to have a cottage in Bickenhill and police parked in a nearby layby. I once went out and said: 'Do you want to come in for a cup of tea?'

That was a dumb thing to do.

They're now disappointed if they just get tea.

Mention scotch and their faces light up and they sit there with the walkie-talkies blasting away: 'Murder in Sheldon' . . . 'Rape in Solihull' . . . and they're turning it down.

One of them brings his dog and I end up feeding that as well. But I don't mind. When Hazel calls 'It's the police, Jasper,' I go straight to the drinks cupboard. And, at least, I'll never get burglars.

That cottage we had was the last house on the flight path to Birmingham airport. People used to call around and always bring their kids, which I thought rather strange. Then the kids would start asking: 'Where's the planes, dad?'

We were so close to them you'd sometimes recognize the pilot. At night the landing lights would be like floodlights in the garden. And there was one Spanish plane, which flew so low that I foolishly rang up the airport and protested.

The pilot obviously took offence because from then

on he seemed to be bent on revenge. Whenever he'd see me he would try and aim his wheels at our chimney.

When we came to sell, it was the only house in Britain with tyre marks on the roof.

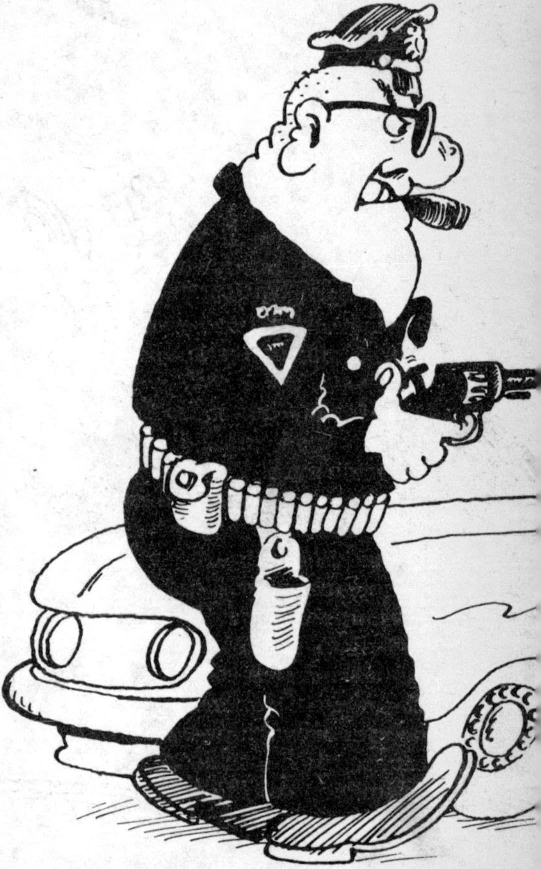

14 American Dream

Rent-a-wreck

Have you ever seen the police in America? All in wheelchairs or with flasher macs or one arm? And when you get there they're like that in real life.

I hired a car from a place on Sunset Boulevard, Los Angeles, called 'Rent-A-Wreck'. A Mustang. Now, there's a fifty-five miles an hour speed limit throughout America. But I thought: Well, if I get caught I'm only here for a couple of weeks. So I'm belting everywhere about eighty or ninety miles an hour – and then the inevitable happened.

A siren so loud it put the fear of God up me. The police car pulled in behind and suddenly there's a six-shooter in my ear.

'Okay, buddy!' he grunts. 'You got your licence?'

I was terrified. I've never had a six-gun poked in my ear before (I've had a few other things). I manage to stutter . . . 'Eng . . . English'.

'Okay! Got your licence?'

'It's in the bag.'

'Okay! Nice n'easy.'

Trembling, I gave him the licence. He puts away his gun and starts flicking through it. 'Hey,' he says, 'hey . . . you're a pretty good driver, huh?'

'Er. . .'

'You sure are. You've been endorsed twice!'

He really began to get interested then, like all Americans: 'So you're English. I've got a friend in

England. Do you know her? Mrs Harris in Blackpool?'

There are so many cars in America. I think it's because of the quiz shows on television. All you ever win is a car. You're sitting in the audience and you can win a car!

'You've won a car, mack!'

'I don't want a car. I got three.'

'Whad-ya-mean you don't want a car? You won one. It's free.'

'I don't want a car ... I want to win the garden spade.'

'Ah, you can't have the garden spade. That's top prize.'

B-o-l-l-o-c-k-s

In California you can have a car number plate licensed with any numbers or letters that you want.

There's this Englishman who lives in Los Angeles who owns a beautiful, shiny Cadillac. He has a nifty sense of humour. He drives around with his Californian licence plate and on it is: 'B-O-L-O-X'. They haven't the faintest idea what it means over there.

The first time I saw it, it sent me into an apoplexy. I was falling about with laughter. The American woman I was with asked: 'What's the matter with you?' 'The licence plate.' I pointed. 'Bollocks.'

'Is that an English word?'

'I suppose it is. I've never thought about it, really.'

'What does it mean?'

'It's slang for Zits.'

It's the only thing I could think of at the time. She believed me, too. She came over here in February and walked in to Boots: 'Hey,' she says, pointing to her face, 'you got anything for these bollocks?'